Florence Lin's Chinese Vegetarian Cookbook

Florence Lin's Chinese Vegetarian Cookbook

by Florence Lin

Drawings by Nai Gi

Shambhala
Boulder & London
1983

Shambhala Publications, Inc.
1920 13th Street
Boulder, Colorado 80302

©1976 by Florence S. Lin
All rights reserved
9 8 7 6 5 4 3 2 1
First Shambhala Edition

Distributed in the United States by Random House
and in Canada by Random House of Canada Ltd.
Distributed in the United Kingdom by Routledge & Kegan Paul Ltd.,
London and Henley-on-Thames.

Printed in the United States of America.

Library of Congress Cataloging in Publication Data

Lin, Florence.
Florence Lin's Chinese vegetarian cookbook.

Reprint. Originally published: New York:
Hawthorn Books, c1976.
Includes index.
1. Vegetarian cookery.   2. Cookery, Chinese.   I. Title.
II. Title: Chinese vegetarian cookbook.
TX837.L49 1983   641.5'636   83-10699
ISBN 0-87773-252-3 (pbk.)
ISBN 0-394-72236-1 *(Random House: pbk.)*

To Dr. and Mrs. C. T. Shen,
for all their
encouragement and energy

Contents

Foreword

We are all faced with urgent and very contemporary reasons for eating less meat than we have in the past. Vegetarian diets have been in use for a long time, most often by those whose religious practice or philosophy sanctioned the right of animals to live; today, there are many people who no longer eat meat, and even larger numbers who have reduced their meat consumption in pursuit of better health and a more equitable ecological balance.

On the average, vegetarians seem far healthier than others. They are leaner, and have strikingly lower blood pressure and serum cholesterol levels. Obesity and high blood pressure and serum cholesterol levels are strongly associated with increased risk of heart disease, our most common cause of death. Some doctors believe, too, that, because of the way it is digested, the vegetarian diet reduces one's chance of getting diverticulitis, appendicitis, and cancer of the intestine.

In addition, an awareness of our growing world population and a commitment to a decent diet for all mankind force us to be critical of meat as a major source of nutrition. The nutrition supplied by a pound of meat costs eight times the same nutritive value in the plant foods the animal must be fed. The earth seems able to support only a minority with the questionable privilege of eating meat as their predominant food.

I can think of no better way to contend with the medical and ecological imperatives to eat a more vegetarian diet than with the wonderful cuisine of China, so well taught by the recipes of Florence Lin. As a beginner who knew nothing of cooking, I found her earlier writing exemplary: it was clear, practical, and detailed.

And what satisfying results! Later, when I studied with her at the China Institute in New York, I discovered why the recipes were so good: they were fine to start with, but then were tried over and over again, and, after many revisions, were as polished and perfect as the work of any great artist. Their simplicity and clarity follow, as with any art, from both intense dedication, and Mrs. Lin's obvious inspiration.

This book should bring much help and satisfaction: good cooking, good eating, and good health!

DAVID RUSH, M.D., FAAP, FAPHA
Associate Professor of Public Health (Epidemiology) and Pediatrics; Member, Institute of Human Nutrition, Columbia University

Preface

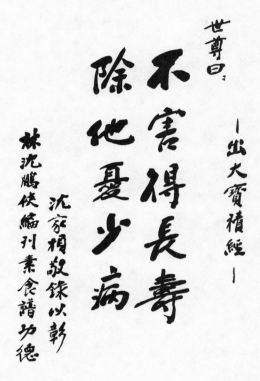

世尊曰：

不害得長壽
除他憂少病

—出大寶積經—

沈家楨敬錄以彰
林沈鵬俠編刊素食譜功德

The Buddha said:

> One will enjoy longevity
>   By not killing or harming others,
> One will seldom be sick
>   If one relieves others' worry and grief.

The above statement is taken from the *Maharatnakuta Sutra*. With such wisdom, Florence Lin has prepared this remarkable book, *Chinese Vegetarian Cookbook*, which will no doubt benefit many people in the years to come.

C. T. SHEN
*President, The Institute for
Advanced Studies of World Religions*

Acknowledgments

Thanks to
Elizabeth Backman—for her unsurpassed trust
and confidence as my edi-
tor
Nai Gi —for her genuine friendship
and artistic contributions

Introduction

For people, food is heaven.

From China's earliest days, food has been an integral part of its culture. Today, in China, food still plays a very important role, both in the daily lives of the Chinese people as well as in the celebration of all special occasions. During New Year's Eve, weddings, birthdays, and dignitary state banquets, food is always celebrated in the form of a feast.

Civilized Chinese patterns of eating were established by Confucius. Later, these patterns were practiced and elaborated upon by other Chinese intellectuals and philosophers who, in turn, created the art of cooking and introduced the appreciation of good food.

Lao-tze, a contemporary of Confucius and another philosopher and great teacher, taught Chinese Taoism—leading a natural life of peace, harmony, and happiness. Taoists believe in simplicity, meditation, and tranquility. They also believe in eating good, natural foods from the earth. Good foods and good health always have been closely associated. The Taoists believed that plants, seeds, and nuts, which are life-giving foods for animals, were good for human beings as well. They also believed that certain plants, herbs, and spices, such as ginger, garlic, onions, and leeks, had good medicinal values. Although their diet was not limited to vegetarian foods, Taoists in their return to nature discovered many edible vegetables, spices, and herbs. These discoveries, occurring in the early stages of Chinese history, helped create the basis of Chinese vegetarian cooking.

The third great influence in Chinese culture and civilization was Buddhism. Buddhists believe that all animals have the right to live and that killing an animal is sinful unless the animal is harmful to human beings. Hence, except in places where vegetables are scarce, Buddhists usually limit themselves to vegetarian foods.

Initially, the art of vegetarian cooking was largely developed in Buddhist monasteries; later, it spread to private homes and restaurants. Today, many people prefer a vegetarian cuisine for various reasons: health, religion, or love of animals. In addition, there is no doubt that a vegetarian diet is low in both calories and cholesterol, yet just as tasty and nutritious. In fact, the vegetarian diet has many advantages over nonvegetarian ones, particularly with respect to caloric and fat content. Furthermore, a well-balanced vegetarian diet does provide all the nutritional requirements of the human body. For these reasons, it is probable that vegetarian cooking may eventually play the major role in Chinese cuisine. And many people believe that the Chinese diet, consisting mainly of grains and vegetables, may become the diet of the future.

Hints for Chinese Cooking

Over the years, a number of my hints and personal preferences have proven useful to my students. Though some suggestions are especially appropriate for vegetarian cooking, many are of a more general nature. For example:

1. For those who are not familiar with Chinese cooking, have ingredients at hand, allow enough time for the dried food to redevelop, and read through the recipe carefully before starting to cook.

2. The first skill that an apprentice Chinese cook has to learn is the proper method of cutting. The art of cutting plays an important role in cooking a well-prepared dish. All ingredients in one dish should be more or less the same size, shape, and thickness so that all pieces will be cooked in the same amount of time. Shredding means cutting into matchstick-size pieces. Slicing means cutting into bite-size slices of 1 × 2 inches and $\frac{1}{16}$- to $\frac{1}{8}$-inch thick.

3. Many dishes in Chinese cooking are prepared using the quick stir-fry method. The wok is designed for that purpose. However, the round-bottom wok is difficult to use on electric stoves. Many American homemakers never use a wok to stir-fry Chinese food. Rather, they simply use a frying pan with a high rim or an ordinary large, flat-bottom pot.

4. Proper storage of food is essential to keep it good tasting; the wrapped dried food usually keeps longer in the refrigerator or freezer.

5. A good Chinese cook never wastes food. By using different methods of cutting and cooking, every bit of food is usable. The right combination of leftovers can be turned into an interesting lunch. Leftover rice or noodles can be used for fried rice or *lao mien*. A cup of leftover vegetables can be used as a complement to another dish or can be cooked with bean curd to make an entirely new dish. Or, simply combine the leftover rice and different leftover dishes, add water, and boil together for 10 to 15 minutes to make a deliciously seasoned rice congee.
6. Homemade broths are useful in making a dish tastier. The combination of soybean, soybean sprouts, tough or wilted vegetables, mushrooms, and bamboo shoots will make a delicious broth. Use this in place of water.

Good Chinese vegetarian cooking encourages and requires common sense, imagination, and good judgment. Hence, the following suggestions:

1. In planning a Chinese meal, particularly a vegetarian meal, it is important to have one substantial dish, such as one with soybean products or wheat gluten as ingredients.
2. In general, vegetarian foods need more oil and salt, because the dishes are blander and also the intake of rice is greater. If one should find a meal to be too bland, small side dishes of pickled vegetables, hot sauce, roasted salted soybeans or peanuts, and soup will add a finishing touch. The degree of saltiness of a dish depends on the type of soy sauce and salt used. I prefer Chinese soy sauce and coarse salt. Most Chinese soy sauces contain more salt than other types of soy sauce and are therefore saltier. Coarse salt is fluffy and, when measured by volume, has less salt by weight than regular salt, hence it is less salty.
3. In vegetarian cooking, it is important to bring out and protect the delicious natural flavors of the vegetables. If one wishes to enhance the tastes of a dish, it is better to use monosodium glutamate (MSG) than bouillon cubes, maggi sauce, or yeast extract, because MSG will not mask the original flavors. However, it is most important that this "essence of taste" be used sparingly; monosodium glutamate should be used in the same manner as one uses salt in baking a cake—⅛ teaspoon to ¼ teaspoon is all that is necessary in a dish.

4. Since vegetables have delicate flavors, it is best to use oils that are bland or have no flavor at all. In my recipes, I used corn or peanut oil. It is best also to use a polyunsaturated fat since it will not gel when placed in the refrigerator. Vegetables contain little or no fat, and a more liberal amount of oil should be used when cooking them.

Please use your common sense and good judgment with some imagination. In a good many of the recipes, alternate ingredients are provided under the heading Variations. New ingredients come on the market all the time, and less popular ones disappear from it. The availability of ingredients depends on season, place, supplies, and popularity. With this flexibility, new vegetarian dishes can be created all the time.

Florence Lin's Chinese Vegetarian Cookbook

1 The Chinese Way of Eating and the Chinese Diet

The cookery of China is characterized by a diversity of ingredients of cooking methods unequalled by any other culture. This uniqueness can be attributed in great part to the Chinese way of eating. Among the cuisines of the West, starchy foods, such as potatoes and breads, are side dishes, whereas traditional Chinese meals always revolve around rice in the South and wheat products in the North. Vegetables, including soybeans and soybean products, are major secondary foods. Meat, poultry, and fish are generally regarded as supplementary foods in daily meals. For vegetarians, fruits, seeds, and nuts are important supplements to rice and vegetables.

Thus, the Chinese diet is basically a rice diet or, to be more exact, a rice and vegetable diet. This is even reflected in the many idioms of the language: the Chinese say *Ch'in Fan* (吃飯), meaning "to have a meal," although literally this means "eat rice." The term *Sha Fan* (下飯) is also used, meaning "to induce one to eat more rice" or, more loosely, "appetize." Literally, it translates to "rice-sending" food. Finally, there is a special term *Fan Ts'ai* (飯菜) which refers to foods specifically seasoned to accompany rice. Rice is termed by some Chinese as the king of foods, a food for all seasons and for every meal. It is true that people in North China eat wheat and other grains as their main staple instead of rice, which grows well only in warm climates but whenever possible, rice is much preferred and, along with the other grains, it is central to the Chinese diet.

Another factor that influenced the Chinese way of eating is social structure. The traditional Chinese family is a large family. It is not uncommon for six to eight people to eat together, especially when three generations all live under one roof. Usually a meal for an average family consists of a soup and at least four other dishes. Among the four dishes, there are usually two to four kinds of vegetables and soybean products. For small families of two to four people, a typical meal may be composed of a soup and two dishes, preferably one with soybean products or other legumes mixed with a variety of vegetables.

The family structure's influence on eating styles has evolved into a basic principle—that is, that a variety of foods should be provided at each meal. It is not only more satisfying and interesting from a culinary point of view, but it also serves a nutritional function: the diversity of food served at each meal ensures a well-balanced and nutritious diet. Hence, a typical meal usually includes balanced portions of grains, assorted vegetables, and soybeans or other legumes.

This variety is further enhanced by the highly advanced methods and techniques of Chinese cooking which not only bring out the color, the natural flavor, and taste of the foods but also the texture, an equally important factor in the pleasure of eating. For example, combining soybean products with fresh vegetables, mushrooms, bamboo shoots, preserved vegetables, and peppers brings out additional flavors, creates new tastes, and increases one's appetite.

Vegetarians have made a major contribution to the Chinese cuisine in that vegetarian cooking provides much more diversification. This may appear contradictory since vegetarian diets are restrictive. But it is precisely the limitation to vegetables and vegetable products that has stimulated the development of a multitude of techniques for cooking. Noteworthy is the extensive use of soybeans and soybean products, a practice which has further expanded the wide variety of Chinese food ingredients and, because of their rich protein content, added greatly to the area of nutrition. Furthermore, as a result of the vegetarian influence, a great many preserved vegetables—salted, dehydrated, and fermented—have been added to the diet. These preserved vegetables also play an important part in seasoning other vegetarian dishes. Vegetarians also eat a great deal of wheat gluten and sesame seeds as well as other grains, seeds, and nuts. And, for the more liberal-minded, eggs and dairy products are also important foods. All these foods give Chinese vegetarian diets more variety and interesting tastes than might be expected.

2 Vegetables

From earliest times, the Chinese have eaten a wide variety of vegetables. Even nonvegetarians eat a great deal of vegetables. Over the years, vegetables have become the basis of the Chinese diet. Long ago the Chinese realized that vegetable dishes are important providers of vitamins, minerals, and roughage and that beans and bean products, which are equally popular, are high in protein.

In an average family's daily meal, vegetables and bean products serve as "rice-sending" foods, that is, they are cooked to be eaten along with rice or buns. Because rice is ordinarily prepared plain, the Chinese, particularly vegetarians, concentrate on perfecting the seasoning and cooking procedures for vegetables and bean products.

Chinese vegetarians usually prepare several kinds of dishes combining vegetables and bean products in different ways, even for daily meals. However, a variety of vegetables and bean products may be cooked together as a one-dish meal with rice. In a one-dish meal, one vegetable usually dominates the flavor; other vegetables and seasonings are added to enhance the taste, subtlety, and texture of the dish. Such one-dish meals are not only esthetically pleasing to the palate but provide complete nutritive values as well.

In the Chinese cuisine, vegetables are usually cooked in the following manners:

Plain. One fresh vegetable may be cooked by itself.
Examples:
Green beans, broccoli, spinach, cabbage, eggplant, or squash

Combinations.
1. Different kinds of fresh vegetables may be combined in one dish. A fresh vegetable may be cooked with other fresh vegetables providing that the combination is a harmonious blend of colors, textures, and flavors. One should use common sense and good judgment.

Examples:
Green beans with mushrooms and/or water chestnuts
Cabbage with mushrooms and bamboo shoots
Spinach with mushrooms

2. Fresh vegetables may be combined with preserved vegetables.

Examples:

Cabbage with preserved red-in-snow

Green beans with dried salted white turnips

Green peppers with dried mushrooms

3. Fresh and/or preserved vegetables may be combined with legumes and legume products, wheat gluten, or other vegetable products.

Examples:

Soybean sprouts with fried bean curd

Fresh bean curd with fresh or dried mushrooms and bamboo shoots

Fried or steamed wheat gluten with bamboo shoots, tree ears, and day lily buds.

The Chinese also eat raw vegetables, but they are usually marinated or pickled. Vegetables are often blanched in boiling water, steamed, or cooked for a short while before serving, hot or cold, with a special sauce or salad dressing. Although raw vegetables or a salad combined with a Chinese dressing can be delicious, cooked or barely cooked vegetables are prepared more frequently in Chinese cuisine.

The most popular method of cooking vegetables is stir-frying. The vegetables are cleaned and cut, then usually quickly stir-fried in a well-heated wok. High heat is used to stir-fry the vegetables for a few minutes before adding seasonings, particularly salt, in order to avoid extracting too much juice from the vegetables. On the other hand, drier vegetables should be sprinkled with water before cooking. In this way, color, taste, and texture are all preserved. Also, all the vegetables or a large amount of the vegetables should be put into the wok at once to prevent the oil from splattering. Vegetable dishes requiring longer cooking times are often braised or steamed. If green vegetables need to be covered while cooking, do not recover once the lid has been lifted; in this way the vegetables will retain their color. Certain dishes may require a combination of methods, such as blanching then stir-frying, or deep frying then stir-frying. Vegetables should be served in their own juices, which retain flavors, tastes, and nutritive values.

In Chinese vegetable cooking the textures of foods sometimes are changed to please individual tastes or for variation. For example, celery, cabbage, and green beans are usually stir-fried to retain their natural crispiness but occasionally they are cooked until very soft, as in the cases of cream of celery cabbage or stewed green beans.

It is always better to use vegetables that are in season, because they are fresher, tastier, and more reasonably priced. The main reason for combining vegetables is to create new tastes and greater variety. Some foods have complementary nutritive values; others add color, texture, and taste.

All ingredients of each dish should be more or less uniformly cut, that is all foods should be shredded or all sliced. This rule is observed not merely for esthetic effects but for practical reasons too; uniformity in size and shape also facilitates the timing requirement when cooking mixed dishes. The only exception to the rule is in the case of heavily seasoned preserved vegetables, which should always be minced, chopped, or finely shredded.

In addition to fresh vegetables, the Chinese are also partial to a wide variety of preserved vegetables. Unlike most canned or frozen foods available in American supermarkets and groceries, which look very much like their fresh counterparts but have much less flavor, Chinese preserved foods generally look and taste entirely different from the original fresh foods. The Chinese use a number of methods for preserving vegetables—natural drying, drying with salt, pickling in liquids with salt and/or other spices. Preserved vegetables also have to be prepared and cooked in different ways to achieve desired results.

Salting, drying, and drying after salting were the earliest methods used by the Chinese to preserve foods. In every region of China, vegetables such as cabbage, tree fungus, and the turnip family always have been preserved, since these vegetables do not grow in winter. Each region uses its own indigenous variety and employs its own preservation methods. As nature endows different localities with different specialties, it is not uncommon that a vegetable found only in a certain locality and renowned for its special flavor or texture will be named after the place. For example, the province of Yunnan is famous for its pickled turnips; hence this food is called *Yunnan Ta T'ou Ts'ai*. In the same fashion, Szechuan is renowned for a special variety of mustard green that is preserved in salt with hot chili pepper; it is called *Szechuan Cha Ts'ai*. Preserved vegetables may originate from stems, roots, leaves, or from all three. They may be minced, sliced, cut in strips or chunks, or left whole. But no matter what form they take or by what manner they are preserved, as long as they are unique, they will probably be distributed throughout China and exported abroad.

Prior to cooking, unseasoned preserved vegetables, such as dried mushrooms, bamboo shoots, day lily buds, and tree ears, are usually soaked in hot or warm water.

Seasoned preserved vegetables are used to create interesting textures and to give a special tang to a blended dish. They are an important addition to many "rice-sending" dishes. It is very important to know how to handle seasoned preserved vegetables for oftentimes a little goes a long way. If too much is used, a dish can become too salty, too spicy, or both; a normally delicious dish may thus be unpalatable. Different regions preserve different vegetables with different seasonings, but the end products generally have strong flavors. So, for an average family meal, never use an entire can or jar all at once; just use what the recipe calls for and store the rest in a rustproof jar in the refrigerator for future use. Preserved vegetables almost never spoil if properly stored; therefore, they can be kept for a long period. However, since preserved vegetables, whether seasoned or unseasoned, have stronger flavors and tastes when they are initially preserved, it is best not to keep them indefinitely.

The following chart lists important seasoned preserved vegetables for general information and usage:

IMPORTANT SEASONED PRESERVED FOODS

NAME	NATURE OF FOOD	SEASONING AND PRE-SERVING METHOD
Tung Ts'ai 冬菜	Celery cabbage. Leaves and stems cut into ¼-inch squares.	Salt and spice. *Tientsin* with garlic; *Szechuan* without garlic
Szechuan Cha Ts'ai 四川榨菜	Large, knobby stemmed mustard greens. Stems cut into chunks.	Salt, red chili peppers, and Szechuan pepper corns.

IMPORTANT SEASONED PRESERVED FOODS

NAME	NATURE OF FOOD	SEASONING AND PRE SERVING METHOD
Yunnan Ta T'ou Ts'ai 雲南大頭菜	Turnip. Large part of the root stems cut into chunks.	Salt, soy sauce; sun dried.
Red-in-Snow *Hsüeh Li Hung* 雪裡蕻	Turnip-top type greens. Stems and leaves cut into 2- to 3-inch pieces or left whole.	Salt.
Fermented Red-in-Snow *Mei Ken Ts'ai* 霉乾菜	Turnip-top type green. Stems and leaves uncut and in sections.	Fermented, parboiled Soy sauce; sun dried.
Canton Ch'ung Ts'ai 廣東冲菜	Turnip. Leaves, stems, and roots tied into a ball.	Salted and dried.
Sour Mustard Greens *Canton Suan Ts'ai* 廣東酸菜	Mustard greens. Stems and leaves, entire plant uncut.	Parboiled, salted, and fermented.
Dried Salted Turnip *Lo Po Kan* 蘿蔔乾	White turnip. Bits, cubes, strips, and chunks.	Salt and sugar or salt and spices.
Hsiang Ch'un T'ou 香椿頭	Leafy green. Buds, young shoots, and tender leaves.	Salted and dried.
Soy Sauce Cucumber *Chiang Kua* 醬瓜	Cucumber. Various stages of growth left whole or strips with seeds removed.	Salt and soy sauce.
Tea Cucumber *Cha Kua* 茶瓜	Young cucumber. Cut into small strips.	Soy sauce and sugar.
Flat-tip Bamboo Shoots *Pien Chien Sun* 扁尖筍	Summer bamboo shoots. Tips of bamboo shoots, 4 to 5 inches long.	Boiled, salted, and sun dried.
Tender Bamboo Shoot Shells *Shun Yi* 筍衣	Tender shells of winter bamboo shoots. Small, thin pieces.	Salt with or without vinegar.
Salted Black Beans *Tou Shih* 豆豉	Black beans with bits of ginger.	Fermented, salted, with or without ginger.

Ch'ao Lou Sun

炒蘆筍

STIR-FRIED ASPARAGUS

1 *small bunch asparagus (about 1 pound)*
2 *tablespoons peanut or corn oil*
1 *teaspoon salt*
½ *teaspoon sugar*
1 *tablespoon water*

Preparation:
Break off and discard the tough end of each asparagus spear.
Soak the tender spears in lukewarm water for 15 minutes. With
your fingers, pick off and discard the triangle leaves along the
spear except for the tender ones at the top. Wash the asparagus
thoroughly and drain well. Roll-cut the spears and set aside. You
should have about 3 cups.

Cooking:
Heat a wok until hot. Add the oil, then the asparagus, and stir-fry
over high heat for 2 minutes. Add the salt and sugar and sprinkle
on the water. Stir and mix well for another 2 minutes. Remove and
serve hot.

If the asparagus spears are not tender, add 1 more tablespoon
of water, cover the pot, and simmer for 1 minute longer.

Yield: 4 servings when served with other dishes.

Variation: Zucchini may be used instead of asparagus. Clean them
under cold running water with a vegetable brush. Cut off and
discard both ends and cut into 1-inch chunks. Cook in the same
manner as the asparagus.

Jo Pan Lou Sun

熱拌蘆筍

ASPARAGUS SALAD

1 *small bunch fresh asparagus (about 1 pound)*
1 *cup sliced carrots*
1 *quart water*

Dressing:
1½ *tablespoons light soy sauce*
 2 *teaspoons sesame oil*
 ½ *teaspoon sugar*

Preparation and Cooking:
The tenderness of an asparagus spear depends on its stage of growth. There is no set rule as to how long a spear should be after cutting off the tough end. Start cutting the asparagus laterally from the green tips down. With a reasonably sharp knife, cut until the spears become too tough to cut. Discard the tough white ends.

Bring the water to a boil, then parboil the sliced carrots for 4 minutes. Add the asparagus and continue to boil for 2 more minutes. Drain well and place in a salad bowl while still hot. Add the dressing, mix well, and toss. Serve hot. To serve cold, rinse the vegetables with cold water, drain well, and add the dressing.

Yield: 6 servings when served with another dish.

Variation: ½ teaspoon ginger juice may be added along with the other seasonings to give extra flavor. To obtain ginger juice, press a small piece of gingerroot through a garlic press.

Ta T'ou Ts'ai Sun Szu   大頭菜炒筍絲
STIR-FRIED BAMBOO SHOOTS WITH PICKLED TURNIP

 1 *large piece Yunnan pickled turnip* (Yunnan ta t'ou ts'ai)
 1 *cup finely shredded fresh or canned bamboo shoots*
 2 *cups finely shredded carrots*
 3 *cups finely shredded celery*
 6 *tablespoons peanut or corn oil*
1½ *teaspoons salt*
 2 *teaspoons sugar*
 ½ *cup water*

Preparation:
Wash the soft pickled turnip under cold water. Cut into very thin slices, then cut again into very fine julienne strips. You should have about 1½ cups, loosely packed.

Set aside the very finely shredded (julienne) strips of bamboo shoots, carrots, and celery on a large plate.

Cooking:
Heat a wok until very hot. Add 2 tablespoons of the oil and stir-fry the bamboo shoots and carrots together for 3 to 4 minutes. Add 1 teaspoon salt, then stir and mix well. Remove.

Heat 2 more tablespoons of the oil in the wok and stir-fry the celery for about 1 minute. Then add ½ teaspoon of the salt and ½ teaspoon of the sugar. Mix well and cook a little longer. Remove the celery and set aside with the bamboo shoots and carrots.

Heat the remaining 2 tablespoons oil in the wok, and stir-fry the pickled turnip for 2 minutes. Add the remaining 1½ teaspoons sugar and stir and mix well. Add the water, cover the wok, and cook for 5 minutes. The liquid should be almost entirely absorbed. Add the cooked bamboo shoots, carrots, and celery, and stir together. Stir-fry for 1 more minute. Remove and serve hot, warm, or even cold.

Yield: 4 servings or up to 8 when served with other dishes.

Variation: Cabbage, fresh or dried mushrooms, kohlrabi, and fresh turnips may be used instead of the bamboo shoots, carrots, and celery.

Kan Shao Tung Sun 乾燒冬筍

DRY-SAUTÉED WINTER BAMBOO SHOOTS

1 12-*ounce can winter bamboo shoots*
2 *tablespoons corn oil*
2 *tablespoons dry sherry*
2 *teaspoons light soy sauce*
½ *teaspoon sugar*
⅛ *teaspoon monosodium glutamate*
¼ *cup water*

Preparation:
Drain the bamboo shoots and cut into 1½ x ½ x ½-inch pieces. You should have about 2 cups.

Cooking:
Heat a wok until very hot. Add the oil and bamboo shoots, and stir-fry over low heat for about 15 minutes or until the bamboo shoots are very dry, but not brown. Sprinkle on the sherry and add the soy sauce, sugar, monosodium glutamate, and water. Cover and cook until the liquid has evaporated and no excess sauce remains. Let cool and serve cold.

Yield: 4 to 8 servings when served with other dishes.

Note: Fresh winter bamboo shoots taste even better than the canned. If they are available use them, but omit the monosodium glutamate.

Liang Pan Chieh Lan   涼拌芥蘭

BROCCOLI STEM SALAD

You can use one bunch of broccoli to make two different dishes for the same meal. Peel off the tough outer layers from the stalks and rinse the broccoli. Cut off the flowerets (include 1 inch of the stems). Use the broccoli flowerets combined with 1 cup of sliced water chestnuts, bamboo shoots, and/or dried mushrooms as a hot stir-fried vegetable dish, such as Cabbage with Dried Mushrooms and Bamboo Shoots (page 18). The stems can be used in this cold salad dish.

> 2 *cups broccoli stems*
> 1 *quart water*
> ½ *teaspoon baking soda (for extra-bright green color)*

Dressing:
½ *teaspoon salt*
½ *teaspoon sugar*
 1 *tablespoon light soy sauce*
 1 *tablespoon sesame oil*

Preparation and Cooking:
Cut the broccoli stems into 1½ x ½ x ½-inch strips or ¼-inch diagonal slices. You should have about 2 cups. In a saucepan, bring

1 quart water to a boil, add the cut-up broccoli stems and baking soda, then parboil for just 1 minute. Drain and rinse in cold water. Dry the broccoli with paper towels and set in a mixing bowl. Add the salad dressing ingredients, mix well, and chill in the refrigerator. Serve cold.

Yield: 4 servings when served with other dishes.

Ch'ao Chüan Hsin Ts'ai　　炒捲心菜

STIR-FRIED CABBAGE

Cabbage usually has a strong odor during and after cooking. However, a brief cooking of this vegetable not only eliminates the odor but also allows the cabbage to retain more of its flavor and crunchiness.

　　1 *small head cabbage (about 1 pound)*
　　2 *tablespoons peanut or corn oil*
　　1 *teaspoon salt*
　½ *teaspoon sugar*
　　2 *tablespoons water*

Preparation:
Remove the tough outer leaves of the cabbage and discard. Cut the cabbage head into quarters, cutting out and discarding the hard core from each quarter. Then cut the cabbage quarters into 1½ x 1-inch chunks and separate the leaves. You should have about 6 cups firmly packed. Sprinkle the cabbage with a little water to prevent burning during cooking.

Cooking:
Heat a wok until hot. Add the oil and the cabbage all at once, and stir-fry over high heat for 2 minutes. Lower heat if the cabbage starts to brown. Add the salt and sugar, and stir, mixing well. Add the water, then cover and cook for 2 minutes over high heat. Toss well and serve hot.

Yield: 4 servings when served with other dishes.

Variation: One may substitute Chinese celery (celery cabbage) or bok choy for the cabbage. In this case, separate the stalks, wash, and drain well. Cut stalks lengthwise into ½-inch strips, then cut into 2-inch lengths. Cut the leaves larger than the stems as they cook faster. The cooking time and amount of water depends on the tenderness of the vegetables. Celery cabbage cooked with chestnuts is simply delicious. Add 1 cup boiled or roasted fresh chestnuts, with shells removed, along with ½ cup water to the celery cabbage. Cook for 5 to 6 minutes or until celery cabbage is soft and tender.

Tung Ku Chüan Hsin Ts'ai   冬菇 捲 心菜

STIR-FRIED CABBAGE WITH DRIED MUSHROOMS
AND BAMBOO SHOOTS

Several types of dried mushrooms are used in Chinese cooking; *tung ku,* the winter mushroom, is one of the most popular. It is a good mushroom, with a strong flavor and a meaty taste. After rinsing dried mushrooms, soak them in warm water in a covered container for at least 1 hour or until they are very soft. They can presoak in the refrigerator for 2 to 3 days. Always strain and reserve the mushroom water for later use, when liquid is called for in the recipe.

1 *recipe Stir-Fried Cabbage (page 17)*
6 *dried winter mushrooms*
½ *cup warm water*
½ *cup thinly sliced bamboo shoots*

Preparation and Cooking:
Follow the Preparation for Stir-Fried Cabbage. Wash the mushrooms and soak in the warm water for 1 hour. Cut the bamboo shoots into 1½ x 1 x ⅛-inch slices. Drain the mushrooms, but reserve ¼ cup of the water. Remove and discard the mushroom stems, then cut the mushroom caps into pieces the size of the bamboo shoot slices. Increase the salt to 1½ teaspoons. Follow the Cooking directions for Stir-Fried Cabbage, but add the bamboo shoots to the cabbage and stir-fry together for 2 minutes. Then add the mushrooms and stir-fry for 1 more minute. Add the salt

and sugar, but substitute the reserved mushroom liquid for the water.

Yield: 4 servings when served with other dishes.

Hsüeh-Li-Hung Ch'ao Chüan Hsin Ts'ai

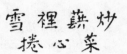

STIR-FRIED CABBAGE WITH RED-IN-SNOW

Cutting is very important in Chinese cooking. The texture, taste, and appearance of the dish depends on size, thickness, and shape of its ingredients. In this dish, the cabbage is finely shredded. The addition of the seasoned preserved vegetable, red-in-snow, makes this dish much tastier.

  1 *small head cabbage (about 1 pound)*
  ½ *cup chopped preserved red-in-snow*
  3 *tablespoons peanut or corn oil*
  ½ *teaspoon sugar*
    Salt to taste (depending on the saltiness of preserved red-in-snow)

Preparation:
Shred the cabbage into 2 x ¼-inch slices, as you would for cole slaw. You should have about 6 cups. Set aside on a large plate with the preserved red-in-snow. Sprinkle the cabbage with a little water to prevent burning during cooking.

Cooking:
Heat a wok until hot. Add 1 tablespoon peanut oil, then the chopped red-in-snow. Stir-fry for 1 minute. Add the sugar and mix well. Remove and set aside on a plate.

Reheat the wok, add 2 more tablespoons of oil, and stir-fry the cabbage for 2 minutes. Add the reserved cooked red-in-snow and stir together for 1 minute. Add salt to taste and serve hot.

Yield: 4 to 8 servings when served with other dishes.

Ch'ao Fen Szu   炒粉絲

STIR-FRIED SHREDDED CARROTS WITH CELLOPHANE NOODLES

  6 *dried mushrooms*
  ½ *cup warm water*
  2 *ounces cellophane noodles*
  2 *cups shredded carrots*
  3 *tablespoons corn oil*
  1 *teaspoon salt*
  ⅛ *teaspoon monosodium glutamate*
  2 *tablespoon light soy sauce*

Preparation:
Wash the mushrooms and soak in the warm water for 30 minutes or until they are soft. Drain the mushrooms, but reserve ¼ cup of the water. Cut off and discard the mushrooms' tough stems. Shred the mushroom caps into very fine strips. Set aside on a plate.

Soak the cellophane noodles in 2 cups water in a saucepan for 5 minutes. Bring to a boil, turn off heat, cover, and let stand for 10 minutes. Use kitchen shears to cut the noodles into 3-inch pieces. Set aside on the plate with the mushrooms. Shred the carrots into very fine strips or, using the large holes of a grater, grate into slivers. Set aside on the plate with the noodles and mushrooms.

Cooking:
Heat a wok until hot, add the oil, then the carrots, and stir-fry over moderate heat for about 2 minutes. Add the cellophane noodles and mushrooms, and stir fry together for another 2 minutes. Add the salt, monosodium glutamate, soy sauce, and reserved mushroom water. Stir and mix well over high heat for a minute. Serve hot, warm, or at room temperature, but do not chill in the refrigerator.

Yield: 2 to 3 servings or up to 6 when served with other dishes.

Note: This dish is excellent in hot weather if allowed to cool before serving, but do not chill the dish in the refrigerator because the cellophane noodles will lose their texture and become mealy, and their color will become opaque.

Cha Ch'ieh Tzu

炸茄子

DEEP-FRIED EGGPLANT

Batter:
¾ cup flour
¼ cup water chestnut flour or cornstarch
1½ teaspoons baking powder
¾ cup water
1 tablespoon warm oil (you can use the deep-frying oil; stir into
      the batter just before frying)

1 medium eggplant (about 1 pound)
2 cups peanut or corn oil

Sauce:
¼ cup hoisin *sauce*
2 tablespoons water
2 teaspoons sugar
1 teaspoon sesame oil

Preparation and Cooking:
Combine all the batter ingredients except the warm oil. Using a
wire whisk, mix the batter until smooth.

Wash the eggplant, remove and discard the stem, but do not peel.
Cut the eggplant crosswise into ¼-inch slices. Cut again into
2 x 2 x ¼-inch pieces. Heat the oil to about 350°. Add 1 tablespoon
of the warm oil to the batter and mix well. Combine the sauce
ingredients and set aside. Coat the eggplant pieces with batter and
deep fry in the hot oil until lightly browned and crispy. Drain and
serve with the sauce or sprinkle with Roasted Salt and Szechuan
Peppercorns (page 138).

Yield: 8 to 10 servings when served as an appetizer.

Note: The eggplant can be fried ahead of time and reheated in a
dry frying pan or on a rack in a 425° oven for 7 to 8 minutes or until
crispy.

Variations: Other vegetables may be used instead of eggplant, such as parboiled cauliflower, broccoli, raw crysanthemum leaves, or finely shredded white turnips or carrots.

Hong Men Ch'ieh Tzu   紅燜茄子

RED-COOKED EGGPLANT

  1 *large eggplant (about 1½ pounds)*
  2 *cups peanut oil*
  4 *thick slices gingerroot, crushed (optional)*
2½ *tablespoons soy sauce*
  1 *tablespoon sugar*
  ¼ *cup water*

Preparation:
Wash the eggplant, remove and discard the stem, but do not peel. Cut into 3 x 1 x 1-inch slices and set aside.

Cooking:
Heat a wok until very hot. Add the oil, heat until very hot, then add the eggplant slices. Stir and turn the slices for about 3 to 5 minutes or until they are soft. In the beginning, the eggplant slices will absorb most of the oil. As the slices begin to wilt, some oil will be released. Pour the fried eggplant into a strainer over a pot. (The drained oil can be reserved for future use.)

Return the eggplant to the wok, add the ginger, soy sauce, sugar, and water. Gently combine and bring to a boil. Lower the heat and simmer for about 10 minutes. During this time, gently turn the eggplant with a spatula. Slide the spatula against the wok under the eggplant, flipping the slices over. Serve piping hot. The dish can be reheated on the stove or in the oven.

Yield: 6 servings when served with another dish.

Variation: To make Spicy Eggplant, use hot bean sauce with garlic instead of soy sauce.

Ch'ing Chiao Shao Ch'ieh Tzu 青椒燒茄子

EGGPLANT WITH GREEN PEPPERS

1 *medium eggplant (about 1 pound) or 4 to 5 tiny ones*
4 *green peppers*
7 *tablespoons peanut or corn oil*
1 *tablespoon salted black beans*
2 *tablespoons light soy sauce*
2 *teaspoons sugar*
½ *cup water*

Preparation:
Wash the eggplant. Remove and discard the stem, but do not peel. Cut the eggplant into 2 x 2 x ⅓-inch slices. Wash the green peppers. Remove and discard the seeds and pith. Cut the peppers into 1½-inch chunks. Set aside both vegetables on a plate.

Cooking:
Heat a wok until very hot. Add 3 tablespoons of the oil, then one layer of eggplant slices. Fry until the slices are lightly browned, then turn and fry the pieces on the other side. The eggplant will absorb all the oil. Do not add more oil since the eggplant will release the oil as it wilts. Remove and set aside. Add 3 more tablespoons of the oil and fry the remaining eggplant in the same manner. Remove and set aside.

Add the remaining tablespoon of oil and stir-fry the green peppers until they are just tender. Push to the side of pan and put the salted black beans to the center of the wok. Stir-fry for 1 minute. Return the fried eggplant to the wok and add the soy sauce, sugar, and water. Cover, bring to a boil, and simmer for 5 minutes. Stir, turning the vegetables, and cook a few minutes longer without a cover. Serve hot or warm.

Yield: 4 servings or up to 8 when served with other dishes.

Note: Salted black beans may be omitted. Add salt or soy sauce to taste.

Fu Ju Tou Chiao 腐乳豆角

STIR-FRIED GREEN BEANS WITH FERMENTED BEAN CURD

  1 *pound fresh green beans or 2 9-ounce packages frozen green*
      beans, regular- or french-cut
  3 *tablespoons peanut or corn oil*
  1 *teaspoon salt*
 ½ *teaspoon sugar*
 ¼ *cup water*
1½ *tablespoons fermented bean curd, mashed with a little liquid*
      from the jar

Preparation and Cooking:
Snap off and discard the ends of the fresh green beans. Wash and
drain. If using frozen green beans, thaw and drain well. Heat a
wok until hot and add oil. Stir-fry the fresh green beans over high
heat for 3 to 4 minutes, or the frozen beans for 2 minutes. Add the
salt, sugar, and water. Mix well, cover, and cook for about 3 minutes. Add the fermented bean curd and cook for another minute.
There should be just enough sauce to coat the green beans. Serve
hot.

Yield: 4 servings when served with other dishes.

Lo Po Kan Ch'ao Tou Chiao 蘿蔔乾炒豆角

STIR-FRIED GREEN BEANS WITH DRIED SALTED WHITE TURNIPS

¼ *cup dried salted white turnips*
1 *pound fresh green beans*
3 *tablespoons peanut or corn oil*
1 *teaspoon salt*
½ *teaspoon sugar*
½ *cup water*

Preparation:
Wash, then soak the preserved turnips in warm water for 15 minutes. Snap off and discard the ends of the green beans. Wash and
drain well. Pile 10 to 15 beans together and cut into pea-sized

pieces. Set aside on a large plate. Drain and squeeze dry the soaked turnips and cut into pea-sized pieces. Set aside on the plate with the green beans.

Cooking:
Heat a wok until hot. Add the oil, then the green beans. Stir-fry the beans for about 3 to 4 minutes. Add the turnips and stir-fry for 2 more minutes. Add the salt, sugar, and water. Cover and cook for 3 to 4 minutes or until the water evaporates. Serve hot.

Yield: 4 to 8 servings when served with other dishes.

Kan Shao Tou Chiao　　　　　乾燒豆角

FRIED GREEN BEANS WITH SZECHUAN PRESERVED VEGETABLE

  1 *pound fresh green beans*
  ¼ *cup rinsed and finely chopped Szechuan preserved vegetable*
   (*Szechuan cha ts'ai*)
  ¼ *cup finely chopped bamboo shoots*
  2 *cups peanut or corn oil*
  1 *teaspoon sugar*
  ⅛ *teaspoon monosodium glutamate*
  2 *tablespoons water*

Preparation:
Snap off and discard ends of the green beans, leaving them whole. Rinse and drain well. Set aside.

Set aside the chopped Szechuan preserved vegetable and bamboo shoots on a plate near the cooking area.

Cooking:
Place a strainer over a pot near the cooking area. Heat a wok until very hot, then add the oil. When the oil is hot, about 375°, add the green beans and fry for about 3 minutes or until the beans become slightly wrinkled. Stir to fry evenly. Pour the beans and oil into the strainer. Reserve the leftover oil for future use.

Reheat the same wok and add 1 tablespoon of the drained oil. Stir-fry the Szechuan preserved vegetable and bamboo shoots for 2 minutes. Add the sugar, monosodium glutamate, and water and cook over high heat for 1 minute. Add the fried green beans, stir, and mix well. Serve hot or warm.

Yield: 2 to 8 servings when served with other dishes.

Variation: Tientsin tung ts'ai may be used instead of *Szechuan cha ts'ai.*

Hung Shao Tou Chiao   紅燒豆角

SOY SAUCE GREEN BEANS WITH POTATOES

This is another form of cooking. The vegetables are cooked until very soft. The addition of potatoes makes this dish tastier and interesting. If frozen green beans are used, thaw and drain the beans and reduce cooking time to 15 minutes.

    1 *pound fresh green beans or 2 9-ounce packages frozen cut green beans*
    3 *tablespoons peanut or corn oil*
    2 *medium potatoes, peeled and cut into 1-inch chunks (about 1½ cups)*
    ⅓ *cup water*
    ½ *tablespoon sugar*
    ½ *teaspoon salt*
    2 *tablespoons soy sauce*

Preparation and Cooking:
Snap off and discard the ends of the fresh green beans. Break into 2-inch pieces. Wash and drain. If using frozen green beans, thaw and drain well. Heat a saucepan and add the oil. Stir-fry the beans for 2 minutes, then add the potatoes and stir-fry for 2 more minutes. Add the water, sugar, salt, and soy sauce. Cover and bring to a boil, then reduce the heat to low, and cook covered for about 30 minutes or until the green beans and potatoes are tender and soft. Shake the pan a few times so the vegetables do not stick, but very little liquid should remain.

Yield: 2 to 6 servings when served with other dishes.

Variations: Soy Sauce Green Beans can be made without the potatoes. Also, Chinese pole beans may be used instead of green beans.

Liang Pan Tou Chiao 冷拌豆角

GREEN BEAN SALAD WITH MUSTARD DRESSING

  1 *pound fresh green beans*
  4 *cups water*
½ *teaspoon baking soda*
  1 *tablespoon finely shredded fresh gingerroot*

Dressing:
  2 *teaspoons mustard powder*
1½ *teaspoons cold water*
  1 *teaspoon salt*
  1 *teaspoon sugar*
  1 *tablespoon light soy sauce*
1½ *tablespoons distilled white vinegar*
  1 *tablespoon sesame oil*

Preparation:
Snap off and discard the ends of the green beans. Break into 2-inch pieces. You should have about 4 cups. In a saucepan, bring 4 cups water to a boil. Add the beans and baking soda, and bring to a boil. Cook for about 5 minutes or until the beans are tender. Drain the beans and rinse with cold water. Dry the beans with paper towels and set aside with the gingerroot.

Make the dressing: Put the mustard powder in a mixing bowl and gradually add 1½ teaspoons cold water to make a smooth, thin paste. Add the remaining dressing ingredients. Add the beans and gingerroot and toss well. Chill in the refrigerator and serve cold.

Yield: 6 to 8 servings when served as a vegetable or as a first-course dish.

Note: Frozen green beans may be used instead of fresh.

Chiao Pan Ch'ing Chiao

CHARCOAL-FLAVORED GREEN PEPPERS

焦拌青椒

Charcoal-flavored green peppers is a Szechuan specialty, usually served as a side dish. It has a crunchy texture and the burnt flavor goes well with congee and drinks.

    4 *large green peppers (about 1 pound)*
    1 *teaspoon salt*
 ½ *teaspoon sugar*
    1 *tablespoon corn oil*
1½ *teaspoons light soy sauce*

Preparation:
Wash the peppers and dry well. Remove and discard seeds and pith. Cut into 1½ x 1-inch pieces. You should have about 4 cups. Put the peppers in a mixing bowl and sprinkle on the salt and sugar. Mix well and let stand for at least 4 hours.

Squeeze as much water as possible out of the green peppers with a kitchen towel or cloth bag. Set aside.

Cooking:
Heat a wok over high heat until hot. Add the oil and stir-fry the peppers for 4 to 5 minutes. They should be slightly burnt. Add the soy sauce, then stir and cook for 1 more minute. Refrigerate and serve cold.

Yield: 4 servings when served as an appetizer or with congee.

Variation: For Spicy Charcoal-Flavored Green Peppers, add 2 teaspoons wine vinegar and ½ teaspoon hot chile pepper oil.

Ch'ing Chiao Tung Ku

青椒冬菇

STIR-FRIED GREEN PEPPERS WITH DRIED MUSHROOMS

6 *dried winter mushrooms*
1 *cup warm water*
4 *large green peppers (about 1 pound)*
3 *tablespoons peanut or corn oil*
¼ *teaspoon salt*
1 *teaspoon sugar*
2 *tablespoons light soy sauce*

Preparation:
Wash and soak the mushrooms in the warm water for ½ to 1 hour.
Drain, reserving ¼ cup of the water. Cut off and discard the stems.
Cut each mushroom cap in half.

Wash the green peppers, remove the seeds and pith, then cut into
1½ x 1-inch pieces. You should have about 5 cups.

Cooking:
Heat a wok until very hot. Add the oil and stir-fry the peppers
over medium heat until they wilt, about 5 minutes. Do not let them
brown. Add the mushrooms and stir-fry with the peppers for 2
minutes. Add the salt, sugar, and soy sauce then mix well. Add the
reserved mushroom water. Cover and cook for 5 minutes. Serve hot
or cold.

Yield: 4 servings when served with another dish.

Variation: Sautéed fresh mushrooms may be used instead of dried
mushrooms.

Chiu Ts'ai Ch'ao Sun Szu   韭菜炒筍絲

STIR-FRIED CHINESE LEEKS WITH BAMBOO SHOOTS

  1 *bunch Chinese leeks*
½ *cup shredded fresh or canned bamboo shoots*
  3 *tablespoons peanut or corn oil*
  1 *teaspoon salt*
¼ *teaspoon sugar*

Preparation:
Cut off and discard the tough root ends of the leeks. Wash the leeks
several times in a sink full of cold water. Keep the stalks pointed
in one direction while washing for easier cutting later. Drain well
and cut into 1½-inch pieces. You should have about 4 cups. Set
aside the leeks along with the shredded bamboo shoots on a plate.

Cooking:
Heat a wok until very hot. Add the oil and bamboo shoots then
stir-fry for 1 minute. Add the leeks and stir-fry over high heat until
the leeks are limp. Add the salt and sugar and stir, mixing well.
Serve hot.

Yield: 2 to 4 servings when served with other dishes.

Note: Leftovers of this dish are excellent to scramble with eggs.
Just combine the leeks with the beaten eggs, and scramble in a hot
skillet or wok.

Variation: 1 3 x 3 x ⅓-inch square seasoned pressed bean curd may
be shredded and added to make this dish more substantial.

T'ang Ts'u Ou P'ien

糖醋藕片

FRESH LOTUS ROOT SALAD

1 *pound fresh lotus roots*

Dressing:
½ *teaspoon salt*
1 *tablespoon sugar*
1 *tablespoon light soy sauce*
1 *tablespoon distilled white vinegar*
2 *teaspoons sesame oil*

Preparation:
Wash the lotus roots under cold running water and peel off the skins. Trim and discard both ends of each link of the roots.

Cut the lotus roots into slices ⅛ inch thick (cut the slices in half if the diameter is large), dropping the slices as you cut into a bowl of cold water to prevent discoloring. Drain off the cold water and pour enough boiling water over the slices to cover them completely. Steep for 5 minutes. Drain the slices again, rinse thoroughly under cold running water, then pat completely dry with paper towels.

In a small mixing bowl, combine the dressing ingredients. Stir well.

Overlapping the slices, arrange the lotus roots in a circle on a serving plate. Pour the dressing over them. Serve cold.

Yield: 6 servings when served with other dishes.

Note: Canned lotus root may be used instead of fresh. Marinate in the dressing overnight, then drain and serve cold.

K'u Kua Tou Shih   苦 瓜 豆 豉

STIR-FRIED BITTER MELON WITH SALTED BLACK BEANS

  2 *large bitter melons*
  ½ *cup salted black beans*
  4 *tablespoons peanut or corn oil*
  1 *teaspoon sugar*
  1 *teaspoon salt or to taste*
  2 *tablespoons water*

Preparation:
Wash the bitter melons and split each one lengthwise. Remove and discard the seeds and spongy parts in the centers. Cut the melons crosswise into slices ¼ inch thick. You should have about 4 cups. Set aside. If the black beans are large, chop them a few times. Set aside the beans on a plate.

Cooking:
Heat a wok until very hot. Add 2 tablespoons of the oil and stir-fry the bitter melon until its color changes to dark green. It should be cooked but still retain some crispness. Remove and set aside.

Heat the remaining 2 tablespoons oil in the wok and stir-fry the black beans for about 2 to 3 minutes. Add the sugar and stir, mixing well. Then return the cooked melon to the wok along with the water. Stir-fry over low heat for 2 more minutes and add salt to taste. Serve hot or cold.

Yield: 4 to 6 servings when served with other dishes.

Note: To reduce the bitterness for those who are not accustomed to it, the bitter melons may be parboiled after slicing.

Tung Kua Yu Men Sun   冬瓜油燜筍

BRAISED WINTER MELON WITH BAMBOO SHOOTS

1½   *pounds winter melon*
  6   *ounces (½ can) braised bamboo shoots with their liquid (about*
       1 cup)
  3   *tablespoons peanut or corn oil*
  ½   *teaspoon salt*
  ½   *teaspoon sugar*
  2   *tablespoons water*

Preparation:
Cut off the skin and remove the seeds and pulp from the winter melon. Rinse, drain, and slice into 1½ x 1 x ¼-inch pieces. You should have about 5 cups. Set aside with the braised bamboo shoots.

Cooking:
Heat a wok until hot. Add the oil and stir-fry the winter melon for 2 minutes. Add the braised bamboo shoots with their liquid, and the salt and sugar; mix well. Add the water and cook, covered, for about 5 minutes over medium heat or until the melon is translucent and tender. Stir once or twice to make sure there is enough sauce. Serve hot.

Yield: 2 to 3 servings or up to 6 when served with other dishes.

Variation: Peeled and seeded cucumbers may be used instead of winter melon.

Note: This dish can be cooked ahead of time, but reduce the cooking time. Later, reheat and serve hot.

Ch'ing Ch'ao Ya Ts'ai   清炒芽菜

STIR-FRIED MUNG BEAN SPROUTS WITH SCALLIONS

1   *pound fresh mung bean sprouts*
2   *scallions, split lengthwise and cut into 2-inch pieces*
½   *tablespoon shredded fresh gingerroot or Soy Sauce Marinated*
      Gingerroot (page 139)
3   *tablespoons peanut or corn oil*
1   *teaspoon salt*
¼   *teaspoon sugar*
⅛   *teaspoon white pepper*
⅛   *teaspoon monosodium glutamate*

Preparation:
Rinse and drain the mung bean sprouts thoroughly. You should
have 5 to 6 cups. Set aside with the scallions and gingerroot on a
plate.

Cooking:
Heat a wok until very hot. Add the oil, scallions, and gingerroot,
and stir-fry over highest heat for 5 seconds. Add the mung bean
sprouts and stir-fry for about 1 minute. Add the salt, sugar, white
pepper and monosodium glutamate, then stir, mixing well. Remove
and serve hot.

The sprouts should be crunchy, so be careful not to overcook. They
should be cooked just enough that they lose their "raw" taste.

Yield: 4 servings when served with other dishes.

Note: To make the bean sprouts look fancier for special occasions,
you may want to pick off the bean sprout roots or both the heads
and roots.

Variations: For Spicy Mung Bean Sprouts with Scallions, to the
other seasonings, add ¼ teaspoon cayenne pepper, 1 tablespoon
light soy sauce, and 2 teaspoons distilled white vinegar. Increase
the sugar to 1 teaspoon.

Chun Yu

菌油

BRAISED FRESH MUSHROOMS

1 *pound fresh mushrooms*
½ *cup peanut or corn oil*
1½ *tablespoons soy sauce or 1 teaspoon salt*

Preparation:
Under running water quickly wash the mushrooms. Just before cooking, cut off and discard, if any, the brown part of the end of each stem. Slice lengthwise through the stem and into the cap, keeping each slice in the shape of a mushroom. You should have about 6 cups.

Cooking:
Heat a wok until very hot. Add the oil and stir-fry the mushrooms over medium heat for 10 minutes. Add either the soy sauce or salt. Stir 5 more minutes or until the liquid evaporates. Let cool.

To store, keep the mushrooms submerged in the oil in a covered container. The mushrooms can be kept in the refrigerator up to 2 weeks.

Yield: 1½ cups.

Note: You can use about 2 to 3 tablespoons of this delicious mushroom oil to stir-fry any cut-up vegetables (about 1 pound). During the last minute of cooking, add about ¼ to ½ cup of the cooked mushrooms to give the vegetable dish an extra tasty flavor.

Variation: The mushrooms may be braised with ¼ cup oil, but cook for a shorter time. These mushrooms with less oil will not keep as long.

Hong Shao Tung Ku   紅燒冬菇

BRAISED DRIED WINTER MUSHROOMS

    20 *large dried winter mushrooms*
     2 *cups warm water*
     2 *tablespoons peanut or corn oil (use the latter if the dish is to*
          be served cold)
  1½ *teaspoons sugar*
  1½ *tablespoons soy sauce*

Preparation:
Wash and soak the mushrooms in the warm water for 1 to 2 hours or until very soft. Squeeze the mushrooms, reserving 1½ cups of the water. Cut off and discard the mushrooms' tough stems. Leave the caps whole and set aside.

Cooking:
Combine the mushrooms and the reserved mushroom water in a saucepan. Bring to a boil and skim off the scum. Add the oil and simmer over low heat for 1 hour. Add the sugar and soy sauce and cook a little longer over medium heat if any sauce remains. Very little sauce should remain when the dish is done. Serve hot or cold.

Yield: 2 to 3 servings or up to 10 when served with other dishes. 6 servings when served as an appetizer.

Variation: Regular dried mushrooms *(hsian chun)* may be used instead of winter mushrooms; increase the quantity to 30. 1 teaspoon sesame oil may be added during the last few minutes of cooking.

Hai Tai Pan Fen P'i   海帶拌粉皮

SEAWEED AND MUNG BEAN SHEET SALAD

  ½ *ounce dried kelps (sea girdle) (about ¾ cup soaked)*
   2 *dried mung bean sheets, each about 10 inches in diameter*
   2 *cups 2 x ½-inch strips lettuce*

Dressing:
¼ teaspoon salt
1 teaspoon sugar
   Dash of cayenne pepper
⅛ teaspoon monsodium glutamate
1 tablespoon soy sauce
1 tablespoon distilled white vinegar
1 tablespoon sesame or corn oil

Preparation:
Cover the dried kelps with plenty of water and bring to a boil. Remove from the heat and let soak for 5 minutes. Wash thoroughly with cold water, making sure no sand remains. Drain very well. Cut the kelps into 2 x ¼-inch strips. You should have about ¾ cup. Soaked kelps may be kept in a covered container in the refrigerator for several days.

Soak the mung bean sheets in cold water for about 1 hour or until they are very soft and opaque. If still hard, soak in hot water. Drain well. Cut up and, if desired, store in the same manner as the kelps.

In a salad bowl, combine the kelps, mung bean sheets and lettuce. Combine the salad dressing ingredients and mix well. Pour the salad dressing over the salad just before serving and mix well. Serve cold as a lunch or salad dish.

Yield: 2 servings when served as a light meal.

Variations: Mung bean noodles (cellophane noodles) may be used instead of mung bean sheets. Soak until soft in hot water instead of cold water. Shredded egg sheets may be added to the salad as well.

Note: Tender dried kelps may be soaked in cold water for 5 minutes or until soft instead of soaking in boiling water.

Tung Ku Hsüeh Tou   冬菇雪豆

**STIR-FRIED SNOW PEAPODS WITH DRIED MUSHROOMS
AND BAMBOO SHOOTS**

6 *dried mushrooms*
   Warm water
½ *cup fresh or canned thinly sliced bamboo shoots*
1 *pound fresh snow peapods (frozen may be used but they will
      not have the crispness of fresh ones)*
2 *tablespoons peanut or corn oil*
1¼ *teaspoons salt*
1 *teaspoon sugar*

Preparation:
Wash the mushrooms and soak in warm water for 30 minutes. Cut
the bamboo shoots into 1½ x 1 x ⅛-inch slices. Drain the mushrooms and reserve ¼ cup of the water. Cut each cap into pieces the
same size as the bamboo shoots. Set the mushrooms and bamboo
shoots on a large plate. Snap off the tips, remove the strings, and
wash the fresh snow peapods. If frozen ones are used, thaw and
drain off the excess liquid. Set them aside on the same plate.

Cooking:
Heat a wok until hot. Add the oil and stir-fry the bamboo shoots
and snow peapods over medium heat for 2 to 3 minutes. Add the
salt and sugar and stir and mix well. Add the mushrooms and the
reserved mushroom water, cover, and cook over high heat for 2
more minutes. Serve hot.

Yield: 4 servings or up to 8 when served with other dishes.

Variation: Canned straw mushrooms or sautéed fresh mushrooms
may be used instead of dried mushrooms.

Ch'ao Nan Kua

炒南瓜

STIR-FRIED SQUASH

Buttercup squash is similar to pumpkin, but the skin is dark green. It tastes sweeter and is much less watery after cooking. The uncut ~~~sh can be kept for months in a cool place. Butternut ~~~ ~~~et than buttercup squash.

~unds)

n cut in half and discard the seeds and ~ash into 1-inch chunks. You should have about 5 cups.

Cooking:
Heat the wok until hot. Add the oil and stir-fry the squash for 2 to 3 minutes. Add the salt, monosodium glutamate, soy sauce, and water, cover, and bring to a boil. Cook over medium-low heat for 15 minutes or until the squash is just soft, stirring twice during this time. Serve hot.

Yield: 4 servings when served with another dish.

Variation: Butternut squash may be used instead of buttercup.

Ts'ung Ch'ao Yu Nai

葱炒芋艿

STIR-FRIED TAROS

   1 *pound small or large taros*
   1 *tablespoon chopped scallion*
   3 *tablespoons peanut or corn oil*
1½ *tablespoons light soy sauce*
   ½ *cup water*

Preparation:
Place the taros in a saucepan, cover with water, and bring to a boil.
Cook over low heat for about 30 to 45 minutes or until tender.
(Cooking time will depend on the quality of the taros.) Let cool.

Peel and discard the skin from the taros and cut into 1-inch chunks.
You should have about 3 cups. Set aside on a plate with the
chopped scallion.

Cooking:
Heat a wok until hot. Add the oil, taros, and scallion. Stir-fry for 2
minutes. Add the soy sauce and water. Cover, bring to a boil, then
simmer for 10 minutes. There should be just enough sauce left to
coat the chunks of the taro.

Yield: 2 to 3 servings or up to 6 when served with other dishes.

Note: Both Chinese and Latin American markets sell fresh taros.
Canned taros also may be used, but just stir-fry them without boiling.

Liang Pan Hsi Yang Ts'ai

涼拌西洋菜

WATERCRESS SALAD

   2 *bunches watercress*

Dressing:
   1 *teaspoon salt*
   ½ *teaspoon sugar*
      Pinch of monosodium glutamate
   2 *teaspoons sesame oil*

Preparation:
Wash and drain the watercress. In a saucepan bring 2 quarts of water to a boil. Add the watercress to the boiling water and let stand for 10 seconds. Drain and rinse the watercress under cold running water until cool. Squeeze out the water and finely chop the watercress. You should have about 1½ cups. Put the chopped watercress into a mixing bowl. Add the salad dressing ingredients before serving. Toss and mix well. Serve cold.

Yield: 4 to 6 servings when served with other dishes.

Variations: If desired, add ¼ cup finely chopped water chestnuts or pressed bean curd to the salad. Blanched fresh chrysanthemum greens or spinach may be used instead of watercress.

Hung Shao Pai Lo Po 紅燒白蘿蔔

BRAISED CHINESE WHITE TURNIPS

The quality of white turnips depends on the season. In the winter they are much sweeter. The amount of sugar and soy sauce should be adjusted accordingly, and one should season to taste. Proper seasoning makes this simple dish delicious.

   1½ *pounds fresh Chinese white turnips* (pai lo po)
    2 *tablespoons peanut or corn oil*
    2 *teaspoons sugar*
   1½ *tablespoons soy sauce*
    ¼ *cup water*

Preparation:
Peel the turnips. Wash and roll-cut into 1½ x 1 x 1-inch pieces. You should have about 4 cups. Place the turnips in a saucepan, cover with water, and bring to a boil. Boil for about 5 minutes. Drain and set aside.

Cooking:
Heat a heavy saucepan until hot. Add the oil and stir-fry the turnips for 2 minutes. Add the sugar and soy sauce. Stir and mix for another minute or until the sugar and sauce coat the turnips. Add the water,

cover, bring to a boil, then reduce the heat to medium-low. Cook for about 30 minutes or until the turnips are soft and tender. Stir 2 or 3 times during the cooking period. Serve hot.

Note: This dish can be cooked ahead of time and reheated.

Yield: 4 servings when served with another dish or up to 8 when served with more dishes.

Hsien Ts'ai Lo Po Szu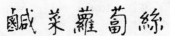

CHINESE WHITE TURNIPS WITH PRESERVED VEGETABLES

1½ *pounds fresh Chinese white turnips* (pai lo po)
½ *cup coarsely chopped preserved red-in-snow or Salted Vegetables (page 46)*
3 *tablespoons peanut or corn oil*
½ *teaspoon salt (more or less depending upon the saltiness of the vegetable)*
1 *teaspoon sugar*
¼ *cup water*

Preparation:
Peel the turnips. Slice them thinly, then cut again into julienne strips 2 inches long. You should have about 4 cups. Set aside on a plate with the preserved red-in-snow or salted vegetables.

Cooking:
Heat a wok until hot. Add the oil and stir-fry the turnips for 2 to 3 minutes. Add the preserved or salted vegetables, stir, and cook for 1 minute. Add the salt and sugar. Mix well. Add the water, cover, and let cook over medium heat for about 10 minutes or until the turnips are tender.

Yield: 4 servings when served with another dish.

Note: This dish can be cooked ahead of time. After adding the water, cook for just 5 minutes. Just before serving, reheat and cook until tender.

nips can be sliced instead of cut into julienne
n chopped scallion can be used instead of
s. Add the scallion to the hot oil before adding
teaspoon salt. Sour mustard greens and sour
oots may be used instead of red-in-snow, but

Tzu 糖醋丸子

SOUR SHRIMP BALLS

tatoes, packed

nced water chestnuts (preferably fresh)

psodium glutamate
hite or black sesame seeds

white vinegar
y
oy sauce
atsup
vater
ugar
cornstarch

ashed potatoes, egg whites, and cornstarch, stirring
n until the mixture becomes smooth and elastic,
add 2 to 3 tablespoons of water while mixing if
Add the minced water chestnuts, salt, and mono-
ate and mix well.

ds and shape the potato mixture into balls a little
he size of walnuts. You should have about 20 to 24
ringly in the sesame seeds and set aside.

Cooking:
Heat a wok until very hot. Add the oil and heat to about 350°. Fry the mock shrimp balls a few at a time until golden brown. Drain and set aside to be refried again. Keep the oil hot.

Heat a saucepan and add 3 tablespoons of the hot oil from the wok. Combine the sauce ingredients thoroughly in a bowl, making sure that the sugar and cornstarch are completely dissolved. Add the sauce to the saucepan, stirring constantly. At the same time refry the mock shrimp balls in the wok over high heat for 1 minute. Use a strainer to remove the shrimp balls and place them in the saucepan. Stir quickly, coating them entirely with the sauce. Remove and serve very hot.

Yield: 4 servings or up to 8 when served with other dishes.

Su T'ang Ts'u Pa Ku   素糖醋排骨

MOCK SWEET-AND-SOUR SPARERIBS

1 *cup combination of diced raw carrots, blanched maraschino cherries, and green peas or another colorful combination of vegetables and fruit such as sweet pickle and pineapple*
1 *large section of fresh lotus root (about 1 pound)*
1 *tablespoon cornstarch*
1½ *cups peanut or corn oil*

Batter:
1 *egg*
⅔ *cup flour*
⅓ *cold water*

Sauce:
¼ *cup distilled white vinegar*
¼ *cup dry sherry*
2 *tablespoons soy sauce*
2 *tablespoons catsup*
2 *tablespoons water*
5 *tablespoons sugar*
2 *tablespoons cornstarch*

getables and fruit on a plate. Peel the fresh
the hard stems. Cut it lengthwise in half,
out ½ inch thick. Cut each stick diagonally
es long. Put them in a mixing bowl. Sprinkle
starch over the lotus root strips, shaking to

ombine the batter ingredients into a smooth
ot strips and mix to coat well.

y hot. Add the oil and heat to about 350°.
alf of the lotus root strips into the hot oil.
minutes or until light brown. Remove, drain,
refried later. Repeat the procedure with the
trips.

gredients in a bowl and set aside.

nwhile, heat a saucepan and add ¼ cup of
wok. Mix the sauce ingredients thoroughly,
e sugar and cornstarch are completely dis-
he saucepan, stirring constantly. At the same
root strips in the wok over high heat for 1
er to remove the fried strips and add to the
the combination of vegetables and fruit. Cook
at all ingredients with the sauce. Remove

up to 8 when served with other dishes.

us root strips may be reheated in a 450° oven
omit the refrying process.

Hsien Ts'ai

鹹菜

SALTED VEGETABLES

5 *pounds fresh red-in-snow or Chinese mustard greens*
¾ *cup coarse salt*

Preparation:
Heap the vegetables in a pile and let stand for 1 to 2 days, depending upon the weather. Turn over the wilting vegetables a few times, making sure they are always stacked on top of each other. Aging the vegetables in this manner will make them more tender and tastier.

Cut off the tough ends of the vegetables. Divide the red-in-snow lengthwise into small sections so that the stems and leaves are still attached to the heart of the plant. Cut the mustard greens lengthwise into 2 or 4 pieces. Rinse well in cold water to remove all sand. Drain well. Spread and dry the vegetables for a few hours. There should be no water left in the vegetables.

In a large pot, place the vegetables layer upon layer, sprinkling salt on top of each layer. Set a heavy object or weight on top to press down the vegetables for 2 days. Turn over the vegetables a few times. Push down the weight as hard as possible so that all the vegetables will soak up the juices which accumulate from the salting.

Pack the salted vegetables firmly into a wide-mouthed 2-quart jar. Pour in the salty juices and sprinkle a little more salt on top. Cover tightly. The salted vegetables will be ready to eat after 1 week (the tender parts will be ready in 2 days). Store the jar in the refrigerator and the vegetables will keep indefinitely.

Yield: 1½ quarts.

Variations: Turnip leaves and collard greens can be pickled in the same manner.

醬 瓜

s

following vegetables or a combination:

urnips or young gingerroot, peeled
ots, peeled
bers, unpeeled

.nd dry well. Cut them lengthwise along the
lices or small sticks, about 1½ x ½ inch long.

:ups cut-up root vegetables and add ½ teaspoons sugar. Cover the jar and shake well
ple piece is well coated with the seasoning.
: 1 hour or as long as overnight.

rill become soft and pliable. Using a good qual-
our in enough to cover the vegetables. Press
ll the air bubbles so that all the vegetables are
y sauce. The vegetables will be ready to eat
can be served as a side dish (small dish) for
.d can also be used for cooking as seasoned
sauce may be reused for pickling or cooking.

gerator in a jar, the vegetables will keep in-

3 Soybeans, Soybean Products, and Other Legumes

Nutritionists have established that, owing to their high protein content, soybeans are one of the most nutritious vegetarian foods. In China, the use of soybeans is as old as her history. In fact, in the old days, the Chinese regarded the soybean as one of the "Five Sacred Grains." Although the specific five grains differed from region to region, the soybean was always included. Soybeans are available year round and at reasonable prices throughout China.

Fresh young soybeans can be cooked like peas, while mature ones can be soaked in water and then cooked in various ways. Also, they can be germinated into bean sprouts. Soybeans are processed into a multitude of forms to achieve a wide range of tastes and textures. These soybean products are so versatile that they can be cooked with many other vegetables in a variety of dishes, including soups. In addition, they are important ingredients in making sauces and seasonings, without which the Chinese cuisine could never have been what it is today.

During World War II, extensive research was carried out by the Americans on soybean-based foods. However, little success was achieved because of what many people considered a lack of palatability. In recent years, however, because of the rising costs of meat, attention once again is focusing on the soybean. Many brands of margarine and salad oil now are being made from soybeans. Soybeans are also the base of imitation bacon bits and strips as well as of an unflavored texturized vegetable protein used as meat extender, all of which are available in large supermarkets. Although these products are useful, converting soybeans into "meat" is unnecessarily limiting. Soybeans should be eaten as beans and bean products as well. With their good natural taste and characteristics, soybeans, soybean sprouts, and other soybean products are consumed all over China and its neighboring countries. In a vegetarian meal, bean products can replace meats, fish, and other seafoods with remarkable satisfaction. While bean curd has been called the poor man's meat, it nevertheless can be the delight of gourmets when tastefully prepared.

To produce their various soybean products through the ages, the Chinese have applied the "wet-ground" method, wherein mature soybeans are presoaked and ground with water. These products include:

1. Soybean milk. Used just like ordinary milk.
2. Soybean curd and pressed bean curd. Very versatile ingredients in Chinese vegetarian cooking, with unique textures and flavors.
3. Fresh fried bean curd. A different texture from the fresh or pressed bean curd, not to be confused with home-fried bean curd.
4. Fresh and dried bean milk skin and fresh bean curd skin. Chewier in texture than fresh or pressed bean curd. As a matter of fact, bean curd skin is more tender and substantial than bean milk skin.
5. Fermented bean curd. A highly seasoned cheeselike bean product used for flavoring or as a side dish.
6. Fresh Chinese soybean meal. Residue from making soybean milk. Entirely different from American soybean meal, it is seasoned and stir-fried to make a side dish.

The other legumes that the Chinese use most often in their cooking are fava beans, mung beans, red beans, and black beans. The Chinese eat fava beans pretty much like Westerners eat peas. When the beans are young, they are used as a vegetable; when mature, they can be eaten after germinating or drying. Fava beans are also cooked in soups, pureed and cooked with salted vegetables, or fermented to make a tasty brown bean sauce. They have a unique taste and enhance any dish with an indescribable flavor.

The mung bean, though not as versatile as the soybean, is the basis for three very important products in Chinese cooking. Bean sprouts, the most prevalently used vegetable in American Chinese restaurants, is the sprout of the mung bean. Also, cellophane noodles and mung bean sheets, two important ingredients in Chinese vegetarian cooking, are made from the mung bean.

Red beans are soaked and then cooked either alone or with rice. Red beans also are mashed and made into red bean paste, which probably is the most important ingredient in Chinese sweet pastries. This paste tastes like chocolate and is used much in the same way as Westerners use the latter ingredient, which is not available in China.

CHART OF SOYBEAN PRODUCTS

Fresh Soybeans 毛豆

Mature Dried Soybeans 黄豆

Germinated
Bean Sprouts 黄豆芽

Pressed
Cooking Oil 豆油
Soybean Meal 豆粉

Soaked, Ground, and Strained

Soybean Milk Residue 豆渣

Soybean Milk 豆浆

Fermented with Flour, Cured in Brine
Brown Bean Sauce 原晒豉 (豆瓣醬)

Spiced 辣豆瓣醬

Ground 磨豉 原豉豉

Soy Sauce 醬油
Light 抽 Dark 老抽

Curd and Whey

Bean Milk Sheets
(Film from Simmering Bean Milk)

Fresh
Fu Yi 腐衣 (腐皮)

Dried
Fu Yi 腐衣 (腐皮)
Yuan Chu 圓竹
Erh Chu 二竹
San Pien Fu Chu 三邊腐竹

Firm Bean Curd 老豆腐

Tender Bean Curd 嫩豆腐

Curdled Bean Milk 豆腐花

Pressed 豆腐乾 Fried 油豆腐 Fermented 腐乳 Pressed Bean Curd Sheet 百葉

Plain 白 Seasoned 五香 White 白 Red 紅 Spiced 辣

Black beans are soaked then often cooked with other vegetables to make soup. They are also made into fermented salted black beans, one of the most commonly used seasoning ingredients in Chinese cooking.

Chiang Kua Ch'ao Mao Tou　　醬瓜炒毛豆

FRESH SOYBEANS WITH SOY SAUCE CUCUMBER

1 6-ounce can soy sauce cucumber
2 cups shelled fresh soybeans
2 tablespoons minced young gingerroot
2 tablespoons peanut or corn oil
2 cups water

Preparation:
Drain the liquid from the canned soy sauce cucumber and cut the cucumber into pieces the size of the shelled soybeans. Set aside the cucumber pieces, soybeans, and gingerroot on a large plate.

Cooking:
Heat a wok until hot. Add the oil, gingerroot, and soybeans, and stir-fry for 2 to 3 minutes. Add enough water to cover the beans, then bring to a boil. Cover and simmer for about 20 minutes or until tender and very little liquid remains. Add the soy sauce cucumbers and cook for 2 minutes more.

Serve hot or cold. This is a salty dish and should be served in small portions. It can be kept in the refrigerator for up to two weeks.

Yield: 6 to 8 servings when served with other vegetable dishes.

Note: Parboil the fresh soybeans to make shelling easier.

Varitation: Fresh soybeans are delicious and can be cooked plain in their pods. Season them with salt or soy sauce.

Yu Cha Huang Tou

油炸黄豆

FRIED DRIED SOYBEANS

1 *cup dried soybeans*
1 *tablespoon sugar dissolved in 4 cups water*
1 *cup peanut or corn oil*
1 *teaspoon fine salt*

Preparation and Cooking:
Check over the beans and discard any bad ones. Wash the beans and soak them in the sugar-water mixture for about 4 hours.

Drain the beans in a colander then spread on a tray and dry for 2 to 3 hours.

Heat a wok until very hot. Add the oil and heat to about 325°. Fry the beans for about 7 to 8 minutes or until golden brown, stirring often. Drain off the oil and place the beans on paper towels. Sprinkle some fine salt on the fried beans while they are still hot. Let cool and store in a covered jar without refrigerating. Serve the beans as a snack, with cocktails, or with congee.

Yield: 2 cups fried dried soybeans.

Sun Tou

笋豆

DRIED SOYBEANS WITH BAMBOO SHOOTS

½ *pound dried soybeans (about 1¼ cups)*
4 *cups cold water*
1 *cup bamboo shoots, cut into 1 x ⅛ x ⅛-inch strips*
¼ *cup soy sauce*
2 *tablespoons sugar*

Preparation and Cooking:
Check over the beans and discard the bad ones. Wash well. Put the beans in a saucepan, cover with the cold water, and let soak until the husks or skins are smooth. Soaking time depends on the size and dryness of the beans and on the room temperature. It can range from 1 to 4 hours.

Bring the beans and water to a boil. Cover and reduce the heat to low and cook for 1½ hours, or until the beans are soft but not falling apart.

By this time most of the liquid will have been absorbed. Add the bamboo shoot strips, soy sauce, and sugar. Gently mix well and cook for 30 minutes. There will be very little liquid left and, as they cook, the beans will become dry. At this stage of cooking, the beans have to be stirred to avoid scorching, but stirring should be gentle so that the beans will not fall apart. Cook and stir for 10 minutes more.

Spread the beans and bamboo shoot strips on a cookie sheet. Bake in a preheated 200° oven for 1 hour, stirring 2 to 3 times. Reduce the heat to 160° and bake for 1 more hour or until the beans become wrinkled and the bamboo shoots dry. Store in a jar in the refrigerator.

The beans are excellent as a snack or appetizer, and go well with congee.

Yield: 2 cups dried soybeans with bamboo shoots.

Tou Chiang

豆 漿

SOYBEAN MILK

1 *pound dried soybeans (about 2½ cups)*
Fresh cold water
Muslin or nylon bag

Preparation and Cooking:
Check over the beans and discard the bad ones. Wash the beans and soak in 6 cups cold water overnight or until their seed coats are smooth and the beans are fully expanded.

Drain the beans, but save the soaking water. You should have about 7 cups of beans after soaking. Boil the soaking water for 5 minutes, skim and discard the foam from the top, and reserve the remaining liquid for soup or sauce bases.

Grind the soaked beans in a blender, 1 cup of beans with 1 cup fresh, warm water at a time. With a large bowl or pot placed underneath, pour the ground beans into a muslin or nylon bag. Squeeze the bag and wring out the milk. Into another pot containing 7 cups warm water, squeeze the bean bag again to obtain more milk. If you wish you may place a weight on the bag to slowly press out the milk over a period of a few hours. You should have 12 cups milk.

Combine the 2 pots of milk and slowly bring to a boil. Simmer for 5 minutes to remove any strong raw bean flavor. (Reserve the soybean milk residue for other dishes, such as Soybean Milk Residue with Scallion.)

To make sweet bean milk, add sugar to taste and serve piping hot or ice cold. To make salty bean milk, season with soy sauce, salt, sesame oil, vinegar, chopped scallion, and *Szechuan cha ts'ai* to taste. This is best served piping hot.

Yield: 3 quarts soybean milk, 4 cups *tou fu cha* (soybean milk residue) and 4 cups soybean soaking water or soup stock (which can be cooked further and reduced to 1 cup concentrated stock).

Ts'ung Hua Tou Fu Cha   葱花豆腐渣

SOYBEAN MILK RESIDUE WITH SCALLION

After making Soybean Milk, the residue, *tou fu cha,* may be seasoned and cooked into a delicious dish. Also, you may combine it with other dishes, use it as a sandwich spread, or put it on crackers to serve with cocktails.

⅓ *cup peanut or corn oil*
2 *tablespoons chopped scallion*
2 *cups Soybean Milk Residue* (tou fu cha) *(page 56)*
2 *teaspoons salt*
¼ *teaspoon monosodium glutamate*
1 *cup Soybean Soaking Water (page 56)*

Preparation and Cooking:
Heat a wok until very hot. Add the oil and scallion and cook for 30 seconds. Add the soybean residue and stir, turning it, for about 5 minutes. Add the salt, monosodium glutamate, and soybean soaking water. Stir-fry for 10 minutes more or until the *tou fu cha* is fairly dry and not watery. Serve hot or cold.

Yield: 2 cups seasoned soybean residue.

Fu P'i Sung   腐皮鬆

MINCED DRIED BEAN MILK STICKS

       4 *ounces dried bean milk sticks* (yüan chu)
       4 *cups warm water*
     ½ *recipe Braised Fresh Mushrooms (page 35) (see Note below)*
     ½ *cup finely chopped bamboo shoots*
     ¼ *cup oil from Braised Fresh Mushrooms (page 35) (see Note*
          below)
       3 *tablespoons soy sauce*
  1½ *teaspoons sugar*
     ⅛ *teaspoon monosodium glutamate*
       1 *tablespoon sesame oil*

Preparation:
Break the dried bean milk sticks into pieces 4 to 5 inches long and put in a large pot with the warm water. Slowly bring to a boil, cover, and turn off heat. Soak for 30 minutes or longer, making sure that all the bean milk sticks are submerged in the water so that all will absorb liquid.

Remove the softened bean milk sticks and repeat the cooking and soaking procedure until all the bean milk sticks have softened. Let cool completely. Drain well, then coarsely chop. Set aside.

Chop the mushrooms; there should be about ½ cup. Reserve along with the chopped bamboo shoots near the cooking area.

Cooking:
Heat a wok and add the mushroom oil. Stir-fry the chopped bamboo shoots for 2 minutes. Add the chopped bean milk sticks and stir. Cook until no liquid remains. Add the mushrooms, soy sauce, sugar, and monosodium glutamate, and then stir and continue to cook until the ingredients are fairly dry. Add the sesame oil and stir again. Serve cold as a first course or hot as a filling in warm mandarin pancakes.

Yield: 8 servings when served as a first course or 4 servings when used as a filling.

Note: ½ pound sliced fresh mushrooms, sautéed in oil and seasoned with soy sauce, may be used instead of Braised Fresh Mushrooms and mushroom oil.

Cha Hsiang Lin   炸 响 铃

DEEP-FRIED BEAN MILK SHEET ROLLS

6 *10 x 14-inch half-moon pieces dried soybean milk sheets* (fu yi)

Sauce:
¼ *cup cold water*
1 *tablespoon light soy sauce*
2 *teaspoons cornstarch*
½ *teaspoon sugar*
¼ *teaspoon salt*
¼ *teaspoon monosodium glutamate*

2 *cups peanut or corn oil*

Preparation:
Handle the dried soybean milk sheets carefully. Broken pieces can be patched. Place each sheet between a folded dampened cloth and set aside for about 20 minutes or until it is pliable and easy to handle.

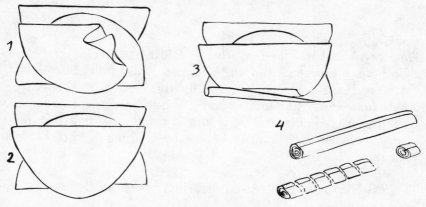

Combine the sauce ingredients in a mixing bowl. On a tray loosely stack the dampened soybean milk sheets 3 at a time, so that each rounded edge is extending 2 inches beyond the next one. While stacking, brush each sheet with some sauce. Now roll loosely, starting with a long side, and roll up the sheets completely. Repeat procedure with remaining set of 3 sheets.

Using a sharp cleaver, chop each roll diagonally into 2-inch-long sections. At this stage the rolled sheets can be kept covered in the refrigerator for a few hours.

Cooking:
Heat the oil in a wok to about 325°. Fry a few pieces at a time for about 3 to 4 minutes. Bean milk sheet rolls burn easily so take them out as soon as they become golden brown and crisp. Serve hot.

Yield: 4 servings or up to 8 when served with other dishes.

Su Huo T'ui and Su Chi   素火腿．素雞

MOCK HAM

1 *pound dried triangular bean milk sheets* (san pien fu chu)
8 *quarts warm water*
2 *tablespoons baking soda*
¾ *cup dark soy sauce*
2 *tablespoons sugar*
½ *teaspoon monosodium glutamate*
1 *tablespoon peanut or corn oil*
2 *4½ x 10-inch muslin bags*

Preparation and Cooking:

Put the bean milk sheets in a large pot with about 4 quarts of the warm water. Slowly bring to a boil, then add the baking soda. Stir for about 5 minutes. When the bean milk sheets are soft, pour them into a large colander to drain. Rinse well under warm running water. Put the drained bean sheets back into the pot with the remaining 4 quarts warm water and bring to a boil. Cook until the sheets are very soft. Drain and rinse again with warm water to remove any baking soda flavor. Put the drained bean sheets back into the pot. Add the soy sauce, sugar, and monosodium glutamate, then bring to boil. Cook until the sauce is reduced to half its original volume.

With a slotted spoon, divide the hot softened sheets into 2 portions and put each portion into a muslin bag. With a long piece of string, tie the top to close the bag, then wind the string around the bag evenly and tightly until it resembles a large sausage. Save any liquid which drains out while tying and pour it back into the pot.

Place the 2 filled bags in the pot with the liquid. Bring to a boil and add the oil. Turning the bags to season evenly, cook over high heat until no liquid remains. Let cool completely, then chill in the refrigerator.

Remove the string and take the mock ham out of the bags. (The bags and string are reusable after washing.) Cut into slices and serve cold. The mock ham may be stored for more than a week in the refrigerator.

Yield: 2 4 x 8-inch links.

Variation: For Mock Chicken, use 2 teaspoons salt instead of soy sauce and sugar. Serve warm or cold with 1 part sesame oil to 3 parts soy sauce as a dip.

Su Ya   素鴨

MOCK PRESSED DUCK

1 *package or 10 10 x 14-inch half-moon pieces fresh or dried soybean milk sheets* (fu yi)
1 *cup peanut or corn oil*

Filling:
½ *cup finely shredded bamboo shoots*
½ *cup finely shredded soaked dried mushrooms (about 6 large,
  soaked in 1 cup warm water—reserve ½ cup water after
  draining)*
1 *tablespoon soy sauce*
½ *teaspoon sugar*

Sauce:
1 *cup concentrated Soybean Stock (page 56) or Vegetable Broth
  (page 135), or ⅛ teaspoon monosodium glutamate dissolved
  in 1 cup*
2 *tablespoons soy sauce*
2 *teaspoons sugar*

Preparation and Cooking:
Handle the dried bean milk sheets carefully. Broken pieces can be patched. Place each piece dried bean milk sheet between a folded dampened cloth. Set aside for 20 minutes or until it is pliable and easy to handle.

Meanwhile, heat a wok, add 2 tablespoons of the oil, and stir-fry the bamboo shoots and mushrooms together for 2 minutes. Add the soy sauce and sugar; stir, mixing well. Add the reserved ½ cup mushroom water. Cook until vegetables are fairly dry. Remove filling from the wok and set aside.

Pull off the hard edges, if there are any, from the bean milk sheets. Do not discard them, but save for other dishes. They can be cooked in soups or Congee with Ginkgo Nuts (page 149).

Divide the filling into 10 portions. Spread 1 portion of filling over a 3 x 7-inch area in the center of 1 bean milk sheet. Fold up the sheet in an envelope fashion into a 3 x 7-inch rectangle. Set aside. Spread another portion of filling in the same fashion on another sheet. With the folded side down, place the first bean milk sheet envelope on top of the filling of the second sheet. Fold up the second sheet like an envelope again. You now have 1 envelope inside another. Repeat until 5 filled sheets are all wrapped together. With the remaining 5 bean milk sheets, make another complete package by filling and enclosing in the same manner. Set the 2 packages aside.

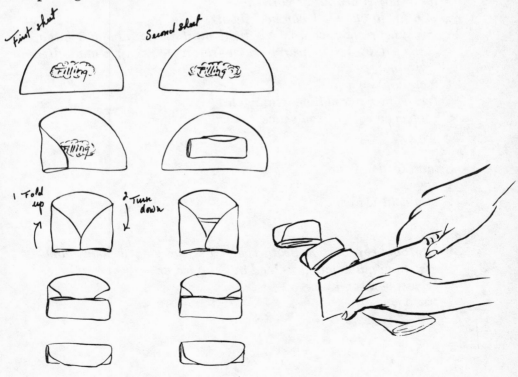

Place a large skillet over medium heat. When it is very hot, add the remaining oil and heat to about 300°. Deep fry the filled *su ya* one at a time for 2 minutes on each side, or until light brown and resembling a deep-fried boneless duck. Remove the *su ya*.

Strain the oil and save for future use. Put the mock duck in the skillet. Combine the sauce ingredients, add to the skillet, and bring to a boil. Cover and cook over low heat for 15 minutes, basting occasionally with the sauce. There should be little sauce left. Chill, then cut each piece into 2 x 1-inch strips. Serve cold.

Yield: 12 servings as hors d'oeuvres; 4 servings or up to 8 when served with other dishes.

Su Fang   酥方

VEGETARIAN PIE

  8 10 x 14-*inch half-moon pieces dried bean milk sheets* (fu yi)

Filling:
  2 *tablespoons peanut or corn oil*
  ½ *cup finely chopped bamboo shoots*
  ½ *cup finely chopped soaked dried mushrooms (about 6 large, soaked in 1 cup warm water—reserve ½ cup water after draining)*
  1 *teaspoon sugar*
  ¼ *teaspoon monosodium glutamate*
  1½ *tablespoons light soy sauce*

Batter:
  6 *tablespoons flour*
  1 *egg*
  ½ *cup cold water*

Sauce:
  ¾ *cup Soybean Sprout Broth (page 130) or ⅛ teaspoon monosodium glutamate dissolved in 1 cup water*
  ½ *tablespoon soy sauce*
  ¼ *teaspoon salt*

Hoisin *Sauce Mixture:*
- ¼ *cup* hoisin *sauce*
- 2 *tablespoons water*
- 1 *teaspoon sesame oil*
- 2 *teaspoons sugar*

- 2 *cups peanut or corn oil*
- 12 *hot mandarin pancakes*
- ½ *cup shredded scallion (white part only)*

Preparation and Cooking:

Handle the bean milk sheets carefully. Broken pieces can be patched. Place each sheet between a folded dampened cloth and set aside for 20 minutes or until sheets are pliable enough to handle.

To make the filling, heat a wok, add 2 tablespoons oil and stir-fry the chopped bamboo shoots and mushrooms for 2 minutes. Add the sugar, monosodium glutamate, soy sauce and the reserved mushroom liquor. Stir and cook until the excess liquid has evaporated. Remove and let cool.

To make the batter, mix the batter ingredients with a wire whisk, until the batter has the consistency of heavy cream. Set aside.

Combine the sauce ingredients and set aside. Combine the *hoisin* sauce mixture ingredients and set aside in a covered dish until ready to serve.

Place a softened bean milk sheet on a large platter. Spread the sheet with about 1 tablespoon sauce mixture, then with about 2 tablespoons filling and 1 tablespoon batter. Place a second, third, and fourth sheet over the first, repeating the spreading of sauce, filling, and batter on each layer. Fold the right edges about a third

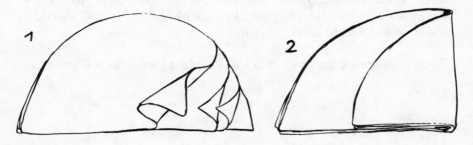

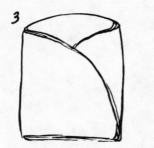

of the way toward the center and spread some batter on the folded flap. Fold the left edges in the same manner. Smear some batter, about 1 inch wide, across the top and bottom unfolded edges. Fold these edges in toward the center about 1 inch, sealing the packet. You should now have a 6 x 8-inch rectangular pie. Spread batter over the entire top surface, reserving 2 tablespoons batter for last-step frying. With the remaining four sheets, assemble the second pie in the same manner.

In a frying pan, heat oil to 250°. Coat the pie well with the reserved batter. Place a pie in the hot oil. After cooking about 1 minute, prick one side of the pie with a toothpick to release any trapped air. Turn the pie over and prick the other side in the same manner. Press down on the pie with a ladle or spatula to keep the pie submerged in the oil so that the frying is even. Turn the pie a few times until it becomes golden brown and crispy. Remove and drain in a strainer. Fry the other pie in the same manner. (The pies can be prepared ahead of time and refried just before serving.)

With a sharp cleaver, cut each pie in half lengthwise, then slice crosswise about 1½ inches apart. Each pie will yield 10 to 12 slices. Place the vegetarian pies in a single layer on a platter and serve with the mandarin pancakes garnished with the shredded scallions and *hoisin* sauce mixture.

Yield: 24 slices: 6 servings or up to 12 when served as a first course.

Tou Fu

豆腐

BEAN CURD

4 *cups raw Soybean Milk (page 56)*
1 *teaspoon bean curd coagulant* (shou shin kao)
1 *cup boiling water*
  Cold water

Preparation:
Slowly bring the raw soybean milk to a boil and simmer for 5 minutes, stirring constantly. (It will foam as the milk begins to boil.)

Put bean curd coagulant in a 1½-quart container. Add the boiling water and stir thoroughly. Pour the boiling soybean milk into the hot water mixture and stir 2 or 3 times with a large spoon. Cover the container and let stand at least 20 minutes or until a very tender bean curd begins to form. Add cold water slowly to cover ½ inch above the bean curd. A few minutes before using, cut the bean curd into the desired size and drain off any excess water.

For a firmer bean curd, wrap the solidified tender bean curd in a cloth. Place in a colander and press with a weight gently but firmly for about 20 minutes, or until it is the desired firmness. The heavier the weight is, and the longer it is pressed, the harder the bean curd will be. Unwrap the bean curd and soak in cold water until ready to use.

Yield: 4 squares fresh tender bean curd, 4 x 4 x 1½ inches.

Note: Fresh bean curd can be kept in a tightly sealed container completely filled with water in the refrigerator. It will keep at least 10 days in the same water.

Chi Hsi Tou Fu　　　　　　　即席豆腐

INSTANT BEAN CURD

Buy Japanese instant tofu (bean curd), and follow these directions to make the quality and texture suitable for Chinese cooking.

　1 *large bag Japanese tofu*
1½ *cups cold water*

Preparation and Cooking:
Use 1 of the 3 packages in the large bag of tofu. Empty it into a saucepan. With a wire whisk, mix the dehydrated bean milk thoroughly with the cold water. Slowly bring it to a boil over medium heat, stirring constantly. Reduce the heat and simmer the mixture for about 5 minutes without stirring.

In a cup, mix the packet of coagulant that comes with the tofu with 1 tablespoon cold water.

Remove the saucepan of hot bean milk from the heat. Immediately add the dissolved coagulant to the hot bean milk, then stir 2 or 3 times. Pour the mixture into a container and cover. Allow it to cool slowly. When the tofu has solidified, use a knife to loosen its sides from the container. Add enough water to submerge the tofu. It can be kept in the refrigerator in a covered container for several days. Then it is ready to be used in any desired dish.

Yield: 2 squares fresh tender bean curd, each 4 x 4 x 1½ inches.

Tung Hao Ts'ai Pan Tou Fu　　茼蒿菜拌豆腐

FRESH BEAN CURD AND VEGETABLE SALAD

This is a tasty cold side dish or salad and an easy way to enjoy fresh tender bean curd. All you have to do is cut or mash the bean curd into small pieces. Season with salt, soy sauce, and sesame oil, or use the next recipe, which combines the bean curd with fresh or preserved vegetables, or even thousand-year-old eggs.

2 4 x 4 x 1½-inch squares Chinese or Japanese fresh tender bean curd, well chilled

½ cup finely chopped blanched chrysanthemum greens, water-cress, or spinach, or 2 tablespoons Szechuan preserved vegetable (Szechuan cha ts'ai) (if cha ts'ai is used, adjust the seasoning)

Dressing:
1 tablespoon light soy sauce
1 tablespoon sesame oil
1 teaspoon salt
⅛ teaspoon monosodium glutamate

Preparation:
Mash the bean curd with a fork. Add the vegetable before serving. Combine the dressing ingredients, add to the salad, mix well, and serve cold.

Yield: 4 servings when served with other dishes.

P'i Tan Pan Tou Fu　　　皮蛋拌豆腐

FRESH BEAN CURD AND THOUSAND-YEAR-OLD-EGG SALAD

2 4 x 4 x 1½-inch squares Chinese or Japanese fresh tender bean curd, well chilled

2 thousand-year-old eggs

Dressing:
2 tablespoons good quality light soy sauce
1 tablespoon sesame oil
½ teaspoon salt

Preparation:
Slice the bean curd into 2 x 1½ x ¼-inch pieces and arrange on a serving plate. Remove and discard the mud and shells from the thousand-year-old eggs. Rinse the eggs well under cold water. Cut into ½-inch cubes and place on top of the bean curd. Combine the dressing ingredients and pour over the bean curd before serving.

Yield: 4 servings when served with other dishes.

Hsiang Ts'ai Tou Fu   香菜豆腐

FRESH BEAN CURD WITH CORIANDER SAUCE

1 *8 x 14-inch piece cheesecloth*
2 *4 x 4 x 1½-inch squares Chinese or Japanese fresh tender bean curd*
3 *cups very cold water*
1 *tablespoon salt*
½ *+ ⅛ teaspoon monosodium glutamate*
½ *cup finely chopped fresh coriander*
2 *teaspoons finely minced fresh gingerroot*
3 *tablespoons peanut or corn oil*
2 *tablespoons light soy sauce*
1 *teaspoon sugar*

Preparation:
Lay the cheesecloth on a large plate. Gently place the 2 pieces of bean curd on top. Pour the water into a 10-inch saucepan. Add the salt and ½ teaspoon monosodium glutamate, and dissolve. Lift the cheesecloth with the bean curd and drop it into the water. Soak for 30 minutes. Set aside the chopped coriander and gingerroot on a plate.

Cooking:
Slowly bring the bean curd almost to a boil. It should take at least 5 minutes. Lift the cheesecloth with the bean curd out of the pot. Carefully transfer the bean curd to a serving dish and keep it hot in the oven.

Heat a wok until hot and add oil. Stir-fry the gingerroot for 1 minute, then add the coriander, soy sauce, sugar, and ⅛ teaspoon monosodium glutamate. Remove the bean curd from the oven. Pour off the excess water in the dish. Pour the sauce over the bean curd and serve at once.

Yield: 2 servings or up to 6 when served with other dishes.

Yen Tou Fu

醃豆腐

FRESH BEAN CURD WITH WINE SAUCE

6 3 x 3 x ⅓-*inch squares fresh firm bean curd*
1 *tablespoon salt*
¼ *cup* shaohsing *rice wine or dry sherry*
¼ *teaspoon monosodium glutamate*
3 *tablespoons peanut or corn oil*

Preparation:
Cut each bean curd square in half, then slice each half laterally into 2 pieces, each 3 x 1½ x ⅙-inch. Sprinkle salt evenly over the bean curd slices and let stand for 30 minutes.

Drain off the excess liquid from the bean curd into a soup plate. There should be about 3 to 4 tablespoons liquid. Add the wine and monosodium glutamate to the drained liquid and mix well. Set aside near the cooking area.

Cooking:
Heat a large skillet until very hot. Add 1 tablespoon of the oil and pan-fry the bean curd, 8 pieces at a time, on both sides, until a light golden crust forms. To prevent sticking, the pan must be kept hot and the bean curd should not be turned over until the light crust has formed. Remove from the pan and immediately drop each piece into the wine mixture. Let stand for 1 minute. Transfer the bean curd to a serving dish. Fry the remaining bean curd pieces, adding more oil as needed, and soak each fried piece in the wine in the same manner. Pour the remaining wine mixture over the dish. Serve cold.

Yield: 4 servings or up to 8 when served with other dishes.

Note: Bean curd cooked in this manner can be kept in the refrigerator for a few days.

Kuo T'a Tou Fu

鍋塌豆腐

BATTER-FRIED BEAN CURD

4 *3 x 3 x ⅓-inch squares fresh firm bean curd*
½ *teaspoon salt*

Batter:
 1 *large egg*
 2 *tablespoons flour (approximately)*

¼ *cup peanut or corn oil*
 1 *teaspoon minced gingerroot*
 1 *tablespoon scallion*
½ *teaspoon salt*
½ *teaspoon sugar*
 1 *tablespoon soy sauce*
⅛ *teaspoon monosodium glutamate combined with ½ cup water*
 1 *teaspoon cornstarch combined with 2 tablespoons water*

Preparation and Cooking:
Cut each bean curd in half, each 3 x 1½ x ⅓-inch. Then slice through each half laterally. Sprinkle with ½ teaspoon salt and set aside for 10 minutes. Lay the bean curd on paper towels to absorb the excess water.

Combine the batter ingredients and mix with a wire whisk into a smooth thin batter.

Place a frying pan over moderate heat until it becomes very hot. Add about 2 tablespoons oil. Dip each bean curd in the batter and fry 8 pieces at a time on both sides until it is light brown. Add more oil and fry the remaining bean curd.

Heat the same pan with 1 tablespoon oil, stir-fry the ginger and scallion for 1 minute. Return the fried bean curd. Add the salt, sugar, soy sauce, and monosodium glutamate-water mixture. Cover and slowly bring to a boil. Cook for about 2 minutes, shaking the pan or gently turning the bean curd during the cooking. Mix the cornstarch and water mixture very well and add to the pan. Gently stir until the bean curd is coated with a light glaze.

Yield: 4 servings.

Huang Tou Ya Shao Yu Tou Fu 黄豆芽燒油豆腐

BRAISED FRIED BEAN CURD WITH SOYBEAN SPROUTS

    4 *cups water*
    1 *teaspoon baking soda*
    6 *1½-inch cubes fried bean curd* (yu tou fu)
    1 *pound fresh soybean sprouts*
    3 *tablespoons peanut or corn oil*
    ½ *teaspoon salt*
    1 *teaspoon sugar*
    2 *tablespoons soy sauce*
    1 *teaspoon sesame oil*

Preparation:
In a saucepan, add the fried bean curd, baking soda, and 3 cups of water. Rest a small plate on the fried bean curd pieces so that they are covered by water. Slowly bring the contents to a boil, then simmer for 20 minutes. Drain, then rinse the bean curd pieces in warm water, then gently squeeze out the water. Cut each bean curd piece into halves, and set aside on a plate. Clean the soybean sprouts by picking off all the roots, then wash and drain. Set aside on the same plate.

Cooking:
Heat a wok until hot. Add the oil and stir-fry the bean sprouts for about 2 to 3 minutes. Add the fried bean curd, salt, sugar, and soy sauce, and stir well. Add the remaining 1 cup water, cover, and cook over medium heat for about 15 minutes, stirring once. Add the sesame oil and serve hot or cold.

Yield: 2 servings or up to 6 when served with other dishes.

Variation: Soaked mushrooms, day lily buds, tree ears, bamboo shoots, wheat gluten, carrots and/or peas may be added to this dish.

Hung Shao Lao Tou Fu   紅燒老豆腐

BRAISED FRESH BEAN CURD

6 *3 x 3 x ¾ -inch squares fresh firm bean curd or 4 4 x 4 x 1½ -inch*
   squares fresh tender bean curd
   Cold water
3 *tablespoons peanut or corn oil*
1 *tablespoon Soy Sauce Marinated Gingerroot (page 139) or 1*
   tablespoon finely shredded fresh ginerroot
½ *tablespoon sugar*
3 *tablespoons soy sauce*
⅛ *teaspoon monosodium glutamate*
½ *cup water*

Preparation:
Put the bean curd in a saucepan and cover with cold water, 2 inches above the bean curd. Slowly bring to a boil and cook over medium heat for 30 minutes. Let cool, then drain. Cut each bean curd piece into eighths and squeeze gently to remove excess water. Set aside near the cooking area.

Cooking:
Heat a saucepan over medium heat until hot. Add the oil, gingerroot and cut-up bean curd. Gently stir-fry for 2 minutes. Add the sugar, soy sauce, monosodium glutamate, and ½ cup water. Cover and bring to a boil, then simmer over low heat for about 1 hour, basting 2 or 3 times. Serve hot. This dish can be reheated.

Yield: 3 to 4 servings or up to 8 when served with other dishes.

Note: ½ to 1 cup Braised Fresh Mushrooms, including the oil (page 35), sautéed fresh mushrooms, fresh or canned bamboo shoots, dried mushrooms, and/or flat-tip bamboo shoots (soaked until soft) may be added to the bean curd.

Chin Chen Mu Erh Shao Tou Fu

金針木耳
燒豆腐

STIR-FRIED FRESH BEAN CURD WITH LILY BUDS AND TREE EARS

  30 *to 40 dried day lily buds*
  ¼ *cup dried tree ears*
   4 *3 x 3 x ¾-inch squares fresh firm bean curd or 3 4 x 4 x 1½-inch squares fresh tender bean curd*
  ½ *teaspoon salt*
   3 *tablespoons peanut or corn oil*
   1 *teaspoon sugar*
   2 *tablespoons soy sauce*
  ⅛ *teaspoon monosodium glutamate*
  ⅓ *cup water*
   1 *teaspoon cornstarch combined with 2 tablespoons water*
1½ *teaspoons sesame oil*

Preparation:
Soak the day lily buds and tree ears with plenty of hot water for 30 minutes. Pick off and discard the hard ends, if any, of the lily buds. Stack buds together, then cut into halves. Clean and wash the tree ears under cold water several times. Drain and squeeze dry. If they are still too large, break them into smaller pieces. You should have about 2 cups. Set aside with the lily buds on a plate.

Cut each bean curd square into 8 to 10 pieces and sprinkle on the salt. Set aside for 10 minutes.

Cooking:
Drain the excess water from the cut-up bean curd. Heat a wok until very hot. Add the oil, lily buds and tree ears and stir-fry for 1 minute. Add the bean curd, sugar, soy sauce, monosodium glutamate, and the water. Cover, slowly bring to a boil, and cook for 5 minutes. Mix the cornstarch and water mixture very well. Gently stir the bean curd then pour the cornstarch mixture over all the pan ingredients and mix until the sauce thickens. Splash on the sesame oil. Remove and serve piping hot.

Yield: 2 servings or up to 8 when served with other dishes.

Variation: Soaked dried mushrooms and bamboo shoots may be used instead of lily buds and tree ears, or the bean curd may be cooked alone.

Su Shih Tzu T'ou

素獅子頭

VEGETARIAN LION'S HEAD

6 3 x 3 x ¾-inch squares fresh firm bean curd
2 large eggs
¼ cup cornstarch
1 cup Braised Fresh Mushrooms (page 35), drained and finely
   chopped
½ cup cooked carrots, finely chopped
1½ teaspoons salt
½ teaspoon sugar
1 tablespoon soy sauce
¼ teaspoon monosodium glutamate
2 cups peanut or corn oil
1 cup vegetable broth or water

Preparation:
In a dish towel or piece of cheesecloth, wrap 1 square of bean curd
at a time and squeeze out excess water. Set bean curd in a mixing
bowl and mash well. Add the remaining ingredients except the oil
and broth. Mix very well and form 8 balls. Set aside.

Cooking:
Heat the oil in a wok until hot and deep-fry 4 lion's heads at a
time until browned on all sides. Transfer the fried lion's heads to a
casserole. Strain the remaining oil and reserve for future use. Add
the vegetable broth or water to the casserole. Cover and slowly
bring to a boil, then simmer for 1 hour. The dish should be served
piping hot and can be reheated on the stove or in the oven.

Yield: 4 to 6 servings.

Variations: The casserole may be lined with a bed of Stir-Fried
Celery Cabbage (page 17). Place the lion's heads on top of the
cabbage and adjust the seasonings. Cooking time is the same.
Soaked dried mushrooms and bamboo shoots may be used instead
of fresh mushrooms and carrots.

Fu Ju

腐乳

FERMENTED BEAN CURD

8 3 x 3 x ¾ -inch squares fresh firm bean curd
1 teaspoon crushed dried chili pepper
½ teaspoon Szechuan peppercorns
½ teaspoon fennel seed
3 tablespoons fine salt
½ cup shaohsing rice wine or dry sherry (approximately)

Preparation:
Set the bean curd pieces between two boards and place a weight on top for 2 hours to press out some of the water. Dry the bean curd with paper towels, then cut each square of bean curd into 9 pieces. Using very thin 5- to 6-inch bamboo or wooden skewers, thread 4 small squares of bean curd on each skewer, leaving some space between each square. Put the skewered bean curd in a covered steamer pot in an airy indoor room or porch for 2 to 4 days (depending upon the temperature and humidity). The bean curd will develop an orangish-yellow color mold and will have a slippery appearance and strong odor. Don't worry.

With a mortar and pestle or a food processor, grind the crushed chili pepper, peppercorns and fennel seeds. Add the salt, mix well, and pour into a dish. Carefully take one skewer at a time and sprinkle the seasoning mixture all over the fermented bean curd squares.

Put the bean curd squares into a widemouthed quart jar then slide out all the skewers. Pour in enough wine to cover and sprinkle the remaining salt mixture on top. Cover and keep in the refrigerator. It will be ready to eat in about a week and will keep in the refrigerator indefinitely.

Note: This is a highly seasoned dish. Serve and eat it in very small portions. It is best as a side dish with plain boiled rice or congee.

Variations: If the wine seems too strong, you can use 2 teaspoons salt dissolved in 1 cup water instead. Fermented bean curd may be made with just the salt and not the spices.

Niang Tou Fu   釀豆腐

STUFFED FRESH BEAN CURD

   4 *dried mushrooms*
     Warm water
 ¼ *cup dried flat-tip bamboo shoots*
   4 *3 x 3 x ¾-inch squares fresh firm bean curd*
   2 *tablespoons cornstarch*
 ½ *teaspoon salt*
   1 *teaspoon sugar*
   2 *tablespoons light soy sauce*
 ¼ *teaspoon monosodium glutamate*
   1 *cup peanut or corn oil*

Preparation:
Wash separately the mushrooms and bamboo shoots. Cover with
warm water in separate bowls and soak for 30 minutes or until soft.

With a small knife, cut each piece of bean curd diagonally, making
2 triangles. Make a small pocket laterally in the longest side of each
triangle, removing some of the center bean curd. Save the cut-up
bean curd to make the filling. Sprinkle the salt on the 8 triangle
pieces, inside and out. Set aside on a plate.

Squeeze dry the mushrooms and reserve the water. Cut off and discard the stems and finely chop the caps. Drain the bamboo shoots, also reserving the water, and chop in the same fashion. Combine both soaking liquids and measure ¾ cup. Set aside.

Mash the cut-up bean curd pieces to a fairly smooth consistency. Add the cornstarch, ½ teaspoon of the sugar, 1 tablespoon of the soy sauce, ⅛ teaspoon of the monosodium glutamate, and the chopped mushrooms and bamboo shoots. Divide into 8 portions, then stuff each portion into a bean curd pocket. Smooth the stuffing. Set aside.

Cooking:
Dry the outside of the stuffed bean curd triangles with paper towels. Heat the oil in a wok to about 350°. Carefully place 2 bean curd triangles in the oil and fry on both sides until light brown. Transfer the fried bean curd to a small casserole, setting the stuffed sides up. Fry the remaining triangles in the same manner, 2 at a time. Drain the oil and reserve for other cooking. Add the remaining sugar, soy sauce, and monosodium glutamate, and the reserved soaking liquid. Cover the casserole and bring to a boil. Simmer for 20 minutes or bake in a 325° oven for 30 minutes. Serve piping hot.

Yield: 4 servings or up to 8 when served with other dishes.

Note: Stuffed bean curd can be reheated on the stove or in the oven.

Variations: Sautéed fresh mushrooms and bamboo shoots may be used instead of dried mushrooms and flat-tip bamboo shoots.

Wu Hsiang Tou Fu Kan 五香豆腐乾

SEASONED PRESSED BEAN CURD

6 3 x 3 x ⅓-inch squares fresh firm bean curd

Marinade:
1½ cups water
  2 tablespoons soy sauce
  1 whole or 8 pods star anise
  1 teaspoon sugar
  ½ teaspoon salt
  ⅛ teaspoon monosodium glutamate

Preparation:
Do not attempt to make pressed bean curd at home in very hot weather; fresh bean products sour easily.

Pressed bean curd is made by removing water from bean curd. To remove the excess water, wrap the bean curd in a piece of cheese-cloth (arrange the bean curd pieces in one layer). Put the wrapped bean curd between two flat surfaces (cookie sheets or cutting boards). Place a heavy object (a stack of old magazines or a large pot with water) over the "sandwiched" wrapped bean curd. The water will drain out slowly. Allow the bean curd to sit overnight or at least 8 hours in a cool place.

Cooking:
Bring the water to a boil in a small saucepan. Add the remaining marinade ingredients and simmer for 5 minutes. Let the sauce cool, then add the pressed bean curd (the liquid should cover the bean curd completely). Slowly bring to a simmer and continue to simmer at lowest heat for 10 minutes. (Do not let boil or the pressed bean curd will become hollow and the texture will become coarse.) Remove from heat and leave the bean curd in the marinade overnight. Drain, cut into small pieces and serve cold, or cook in other dishes.

Yield: 12 servings as an appetizer.

Note: Seasoned pressed bean curd may be kept covered and refrigerated in its marinade for up to 2 weeks.

Tou Fu Kan Ch'ao Ma Ku P'ien   豆腐乾炒蔴菇片
SEASONED PRESSED BEAN CURD WITH FRESH MUSHROOMS

2   3 x 3 x ⅓-inch squares homemade Seasoned Pressed Bean Curd
    (page 80) or ready-made
½   pound fresh mushrooms
2   tablespoons peanut or corn oil
1   tablespoon light soy sauce
½   teaspoon salt
½   teaspoon sugar
2   tablespoon water

Preparation:
Cut each bean curd square in half, then thinly slice into pieces ⅟₁₆
inch thick. Put the sliced bean curd on a plate and set aside. Slice
the fresh mushrooms and set aside with the bean curd.

Cooking:
Heat a wok until very hot. Add the oil and stir-fry the mushrooms
until soft. Add the sliced pressed bean curd. Stir together for 1
minute. Add the soy sauce, salt, sugar and water. Cover and cook
for 2 more minutes. Serve hot or warm.

Yield: 4 servings or up to 6 when served with other dishes.

Note: The pressed bean curd may be kept in the refrigerator up to
2 weeks if soaked in a solution of 2 teaspoons salt or 2 tablespoons
soy sauce in 2 cups water.

Ch'ao Chiang

炒 醬

SPICY CHIANG

10 *dried mushrooms*
1½ *cups warm water*
  4 *3 x 3 x ⅓-inch squares homemade Seasoned Pressed Bean
       Curd (page 80) or ready-made*
  2 *green peppers*
  1 *cup diced bamboo shoots*
  ½ *cup skinless peanuts*
  5 *tablespoons peanut or corn oil*
  ¼ *cup brown bean sauce or 2 tablespoons brown bean sauce
       combined with 2 tablespoons hot bean sauce*
  3 *tablespoons* hoisin *sauce*
  ¼ *teaspoon monosodium glutamate*

Preparation:
Wash the mushrooms and soak in the warm water for 30 minutes.
Drain, but reserve 1 cup of the mushroom water. Cut off and discard the stems. Dice each mushroom cap into ¼-inch pieces. You
should have about 1 cup. Cut the pressed bean curd pieces into
dice the same size as the mushrooms and set aside with the mushrooms.

Wash the green peppers. Remove the seeds and pith, and dice
into ¼-inch pieces. You should have about 1½ cups. Cut the
bamboo shoots into dice the same size as the peppers and set aside
these 2 ingredients on a plate with the peanuts.

Cooking:
Heat a wok until hot. Add 2 tablespoons of the oil and stir-fry the
green peppers, bamboo shoots, and peanuts for 3 to 4 minutes or
until the peppers are dark green and well cooked. Remove these
ingredients and set aside.

Add the remaining oil to the wok and heat. Stir-fry the bean curd
and mushrooms for 2 minutes. Add the brown bean sauce, *hoisin*
sauce, monosodium glutamate, green peppers, bamboo shoots, and
peanuts and stir some more. Add the reserved mushroom water
and bring to a boil. Cook uncovered over low heat for 15 minutes.
Stir, turning ingredients a few times during cooking. Serve hot or
cold. This dish can be refrigerated for up to 2 weeks.

Yield: 8 servings or up to 12 when served with other dishes.

Note: Spicy Chiang is delicious as a sandwich filling.

Variations: Seasoned wheat gluten or soy steaks may be used instead of seasoned pressed bean curd.

Ma Yu San Szu

蔴 油 三 絲

CARROTS AND CELERY WITH SEASONED PRESSED BEAN CURD

The ingredients in this dish must be cut into very fine julienne strips, not more than 2 inches long. The sesame oil and wine add extra flavor.

2 *cups fine julienne of carrots, loosely packed*
2 *cups fine julienne of celery, loosely packed*
2 *3 x 3 x ⅓-inch squares homemade Seasoned Pressed Bean Curd*
    (page 80) or ready-made, cut into fine julienne strips (about
    2 cups)
3 *tablespoons sesame oil*
1 *teaspoon salt*
⅛ *teaspoon monosodium glutamate*
1 *tablespoon* shaohsing *rice wine or dry sherry*

Preparation:
Put carrots, celery, and pressed bean curd on a large plate near the cooking area.

Cooking:
Heat a wok until hot. Add 1 teaspoon of the sesame oil and then the bean curd. Stir-fry for 1 minute. Remove and set aside. Add the remaining sesame oil to the wok and heat. Add the carrots and celery and stir-fry for 3 minutes. Add the salt and stir, mixing well. Add the cooked bean curd and monosodium glutamate. Mix with the vegetables, heating thoroughly. Sprinkle the wine around the edge of the wok. Mix well and remove. This dish can be served hot or at room temperature.

Yield: 4 servings or up to 8 when served with other dishes.

Ch'in Ts'ai Pan Kan Szu   芹 菜 拌 乾 絲

CELERY WITH SEASONED PRESSED BEAN CURD SALAD

1 *small stalk celery or 2 celery hearts*
2 *3 x 3 x ⅓-inch squares homemade Seasoned Pressed Bean Curd
   (page 80) or ready-made*

Dressing:
2 *tablespoons light soy sauce*
1 *tablespoon sesame oil*
1 *teaspoon sugar*
½ *teaspoon salt*
⅛ *teaspoon monosodium glutamate*

Preparation:
Scrape off the outer layer of each celery rib. Break the ribs in half and pull off any strings. Wash, drain, and dry well. Cut the celery crosswise into very thin slices. You shoud have about 4 cups. Put in a salad bowl.

Slice through the pressed bean curd laterally, making layers ¹⁄₁₆ inch thick. Cut again into fine julienne strips. You should have about 2 cups. Combine with the celery.

Combine the dressing ingredients. Mix well until the sugar and salt are completely dissolved in the soy sauce. Pour the dressing over the salad and mix thoroughly just before serving.

Yield: 4 servings when served with other dishes.

Variations: 2 tablespoons finely shredded Szechuan preserved vegetable (*Szechuan cha ts'ai*) may be added to give a tang to this dish. If it is too salty, reduce the amount of salt in the dressing. The pressed bean curd may be cut into 1-inch squares and the celery into slices ¼ inch thick. Stir-fry with 2 tablespoons oil, add the above dressing plus ¼ cup water, cover, and cook for 10 minutes. Serve hot. Also, plain pressed bean curd may be used. After the bean curd is cut up, pour over it enough boiling water to cover, then let cool and drain off the water. Repeat the boiling water treatment 3 more times. Let cool to slightly warm. It is now ready to mix with the celery. Adjust the dressing to taste.

Lan Hua Tou Fu Kan

蘭花豆腐乾

BASKET-WEAVE PRESSED BEAN CURD

6 3 x 3 x ⅓-inch squares plain pressed bean curd
1 *cup peanut or corn oil*

Marinade:
¼ *cup soy sauce*
1 *whole or 8 pods star anise*
1 *tablespoon sugar*
¼ *teaspoon monosodium glutamate*

Preparation:
Carefully score each piece of pressed bean curd at ⅛-inch intervals. Do not cut through; each piece should be intact. (To prevent
cutting through: place the bean curd on a cutting surface. Stack 2
ice cream sticks, or the like, at two opposite sides of the bean curd.
Cut through the bean curd only as deep as the sticks are high.)
Turn each piece over and score again, at a slight angle to the first.
When the pressed bean curd is scored on both sides, it can be
stretched to at least twice its original width and pushed back to the
original size.

Combine the marinade ingredients in a frying pan with a cover
and set near the cooking area.

Cooking:
Heat a skillet until very hot. Add about 1 inch of oil and heat to
350°. Gently stretch the scored pressed bean curd and place in the
oil. Fry for about 1 minute on each side, keeping the scored bean
curd stretched with chopsticks or a spatula while frying. Keep the
bean curd stretched until it remains in that shape and has an inter-
woven appearance, like basketry. Put into the skillet with the
marinade as soon as it is fried and fry the remaining pieces in the
same manner.

Add enough water to the frying pan to cover the fried bean curd.
Cover and slowly bring to simmer. Cook for about 1 hour. There
will be very little sauce left. Serve hot or cold.

Yield: 4 servings or up to 8 when served with other dishes. 12 servings as an appetizer.

Variation: Seasoned pressed bean curd may be used instead of plain pressed bean curd.

Note: If you want a more softly textured bean curd, soak the bean curd after deep frying in a mixture of 2 teaspoons baking soda and 4 cups boiling water for 20 minutes. Rinse several times to remove any baking soda taste, then cook with the marinade and water.

Hsüeh Li Hung Ch'ao Pai Yeh   雪裡蕻炒百葉

FRESH BEAN CURD SHEETS WITH PRESERVED VEGETABLES

Following are two recipes for *pai yeh* (fresh bean curd sheet). They are more substantial dishes and therefore are usually served with one or two vegetable dishes.

1 *8-ounce package fresh bean curd sheets* (pai yeh), 5 10 x 10-*inch sheets*
6 *cups water*
2 *teaspoons baking soda*
5 *tablespoons peanut or corn oil*
1 *7-ounce can preserved red-in-snow, finely chopped (measure the liquid and add enough water to make ½ cup)*

Preparation:
Cut the bean curd sheets into 2½ x ¼-inch strips. In a large saucepan bring the water to a boil, then remove from heat. Add the baking soda, mix well to dissolve, then add the cut-up bean curd sheets and soak for about 20 minutes, depending on the thickness and freshness of the sheets. Make sure the sheets are totally submerged. Stir around to soak them evenly. When they turn a creamy color, rinse several times with warm water. Drain and set aside.

Cooking:
Heat a wok until hot. Add the oil and stir-fry the red-in-snow for 2 minutes, then add the bean curd sheets and stir together. Add the

reserved diluted red-in-snow liquid and cook for about 5 minutes. Turn and stir a few times. There should be very little liquid left. Serve hot or cold.

Yield: 6 servings or up to 10 when served with other dishes.

Variations: 6 large soaked and shredded dried mushrooms may be added to make this dish tastier; adjust the seasonings. Homemade Salted Vegetables (page 46) may be used instead of preserved red-in-snow. Soaked dried bean milk pieces *(erh chu)* or Seasoned Pressed Bean Curd (page 80) may be used instead of bean curd sheets; omit the baking soda soaking.

Pai Yeh Pao   百 葉 包

BEAN CURD SHEET ROLLS

1 *package fresh bean curd sheets* (pai yeh), 5 10 x 10-*inch sheets*
1 *tablespoon baking soda*
1 *tablespoon salt*

Filling:
4 *large dried mushrooms*
1 *cup warm water*
½ *cup finely chopped bamboo shoots*
2 *bunches watercress or 1 pound fresh spinach*
3 *tablespoons peanut or corn oil*
1½ *teaspoons salt*
½ *teaspoon sugar*
1 *teaspoon sesame oil*

2 *cups clear Soybean Sprout Broth (page 130) or 2 cups water with ¼ teaspoon monosodium glutamate*

Preparation:
In a large saucepan bring 3 quarts of water to a boil. Remove from heat, add the baking soda, and mix well to dissolve. Cut each bean curd sheet into 4 triangles (a total of 20 triangles). Add one by one to the soda water mixture and soak for 10 to 15 minutes depend-

ing on the thickness and freshness of the sheets. Make sure the sheets are totally submerged. Gently stir the sheets around in the saucepan to soak them evenly. The sheets should become lighter in color. Have a large pot of cold water ready. When the sheets become creamy in color, gently transfer them, one by one, to the cold water. Let soak for 2 minutes, then transfer to another pot of fresh water containing the tablespoon of salt. (Salted water helps the sheets retain their shape.) Leave the sheets in the salted water while making the filling.

Wash the mushrooms and soak in the warm water for 30 minutes or until soft. Drain the mushrooms, but reserve the water. Cut off and discard the stems. Finely chop the mushroom caps. Set aside on a plate with the chopped bamboo shoots.

Blanch the watercress or spinach in boiling water for 5 seconds. Drain and rinse under cold water. Squeeze out the excess water and chop the greens finely. Set aside with the mushrooms and bamboo shoots.

Cooking the Filling:
Heat a wok until hot. Add the oil, then the bamboo shoots and mushrooms. Stir-fry for 2 minutes. Add the mushroom water and bring to a boil. Cook until the ingredients are fairly dry. Add the salt and sugar and mix well. Add the chopped greens and sesame oil, combine, but do not cook. Remove and set aside.

Wrapping and Cooking:
Place 1 bean curd sheet on a plate. Shape about 2 tablespoons of filling into a 3-inch-long sausagelike shape at the lower corner.

Fold the two side corners inward to overlap the filling. Now roll the sheet up like a 3-inch-long egg roll. Set aside on a plate. Wrap the remaining sheets in the same manner. If there are some torn sheets, just patch them with other broken pieces. (Twenty sheets should make about 16 bean curd rolls.)

With a piece of string, tie 4 bean curd sheet rolls together into a bundle. Repeat process with remaining bean curd rolls. With a little oil, pan-fry the bean curd roll bundles in a heated wok or skillet with a nonstick surface until all sides are slightly brown. (The frying process is optional and may be omitted.) Place the bundles into the soybean sprout broth and simmer for 15 minutes. Untie the bundles. Serve hot with the broth, or cold without the broth.

Yield: 16 bean curd sheet rolls.

Variation: To make the famous street vendor's dish, Bean Curd Sheet Rolls with Fried Bean Curd and Cellophane Noodle Soup, add 6 fried bean curd pieces and 2 ounces cellophane noodles to the broth along with the bean curd sheet rolls. Adjust the seasonings accordingly.

Pai Chu Ts'an Tou 白煮蠶豆

BRAISED FRESH FAVA BEANS

The Chinese are very fond of fava beans. The beans are eaten in all their stages of maturity and can be cooked in many different ways. When the beans are still green, they can be added to a stir-fried dish as a complementary vegetable. When they are dried, they can be used for soups, or pureed. Fava beans are grown in Eastern China and are very often cooked with preserved red-in-snow or with Cantonese pickled mustard greens. The latter is sour and its tartness gives the dish a different flavor.

2 *cups shelled fresh fava beans (about 2 pounds in pods)*
1 *cup water*
2 *tablespoons peanut or corn oil*
2 *teaspoons salt*
2 *teaspoons sugar*

Preparation:
Lightly split the seed coat of each fava bean with your fingernails or a paring knife. Put the slit beans in a stainless steel saucepan along with the remaining ingredients. Bring to a boil, cover, and cook over medium heat for 10 to 15 minutes or until the seed coats and beans are soft. Serve hot.

Yield: 4 servings or up to 8 when served with other dishes.

Tou Pan Sha　　　　　酸菜．鹹菜豆瓣酥

PUREE OF FAVA BEANS

    Cold water
1 *cup dried fava beans, with or without seed coats*
½ *cup chopped pickled mustard greens or preserved red-in-snow*
4 *tablespoons peanut or corn oil*
1 *teaspoon sugar (use ½ teaspoon with red-in-snow)*
½ *teaspoon salt or to taste*

Preparation:
Soak the dried fava beans in cold water overnight or until they are soft enough to remove the seed coats. (Both the peeled or unpeeled beans can be kept in water in the refrigerator for days. One cup dried fava beans makes 2 cups soaked beans.)

Rinse the peeled fava beans in cold water and put in a saucepan. Add 2 cups cold water and bring to boil. Cover and simmer for 30 minutes or until the beans are very soft. Drain the beans but reserve at least ½ cup of the broth. (Any remaining bean liquid may be reserved for soup stock.) Mash the beans into a puree. Set aside.

Cooking:
Heat a wok. Add 1 tablespoon of the oil and stir-fry the preserved vegetables for 1 minute. Add the sugar, stir, and cook some more. Remove and set aside.

Reheat the wok. Add the remaining oil and stir-fry the bean puree for 2 minutes. Add the salt and stir, mixing well. Add the preserved vegetables and the reserved bean liquid. Cook over medium heat for 2 to 3 minutes, stirring constantly. Bean puree burns easily. Serve hot, warm, or cold.

Yield: 4 servings or up to 8 when served with other dishes.

Variations: When fresh fava beans are used, reduce the cooking time and cook until the beans are very soft. Dried split green peas are a good substitute for the dried fava beans. There is no need to soak them, just cook to soften. Good sauerkraut, which is actually pickled cabbage, may be used in place of the pickled mustard green. Japanese salted mustard greens, sold in a sealed plastic bag, is also a good substitute for these two preserved vegetables.

Ts'ao Ku Ts'an Tou   草 菇 蠶 豆

LIMA BEANS WITH STRAW MUSHROOMS

1½ *cups parboiled fresh lima beans or 1 9-ounce box frozen lima*
       beans
   1 *15-ounce can straw mushrooms (reserve liquid)*
   3 *tablespoons peanut or corn oil*
   1 *teaspoon salt*
   ½ *teaspoon sugar*
   2 *teaspoons cornstarch combined with 2 tablespoons liquid from*
       the canned mushrooms

Preparation:
If using frozen lima beans, thaw and drain them. Drain the canned mushrooms, reserving the liquid. Set aside the lima beans and mushrooms on a plate.

Cooking:
Heat a saucepan. Add the oil and stir-fry the lima beans and straw mushrooms for 2 minutes. Add the salt and sugar and mix well. Add ½ cup of the reserved liquid from the canned mushrooms and bring to a boil. Mix the dissolved cornstarch mixture well then stir into the saucepan, cooking until the sauce boils and thickens. Serve hot.

Yield: 4 to 8 servings when served with other dishes.

Variation: Fresh fava beans have a better flavor and texture than lima beans. Remove pods and seed coats. Cook in the same manner but for a longer time and until tender.

Fa Tou Ya   發豆芽

HOW TO SPROUT MUNG BEANS AND SOYBEANS

During the winter when fresh vegetables are scarce, dried mature mung beans, soybeans, and fava bean sprouts make delicious substitutes. (Fava beans will be discussed in the next recipe.) Winter sprouts are actually better than summer sprouts. The quality and freshness of the dried beans has much to do with the resulting sprouts. In other words, a new crop of beans of highest quality is much preferred.

Mung Bean Sprouts: For small quantities, soak ½ cup well washed mung beans in 2 cups warm water for 6 to 8 hours then rinse with cold water. Put the beans in a plastic bag with many small holes punched in the bottom and sides for drainage. On top of the beans lay four layers of terrycloth (a folded towel, for example) to provide weight and humidity and hold moisture. This makes for fatter, juicier sprouts. Set the plastic bag on a colander or a rack in a large pot. The beans sprout best in a dark, damp place. During the fall, winter, and spring, when room temperature is usually around 70° (an ideal temperature for high quality sprouts), store the beans under the sink or in the bathroom or closet. During the summer when room temperature is too high, basement temperature may be satisfactory.

Thoroughly rinse the beans 3 or 4 times a day by filling the plastic bag with tap water and without removing the folded towel. Do not let the beans remain without rinsing longer than 8 hours. In 3 to 4 days, depending on the temperature, the beans will develop white sprouts which should be 2 to 3 inches long, sturdy, and firm. The yellow plumule of the beans will just come out. (Half a cup of dried mung beans yields 2 pounds or 14 cups of sprouts.) Rinse the bean sprouts in a sinkful of cold water. Most of the green seed coats will float to the top; remove and discard them. Pick up the mung bean sprouts by the handful and drain well. Cleaned sprouts can be kept in a plastic bag in the refrigerator for a few days.

For quick stir-fried mung bean sprouts see page 34. For a salad, dip in boiling water for 5 seconds then rinse with cold water and drain well. A dressing containing vinegar is best.

Soybean Sprouts: Soybeans will spoil easily during sprouting; so use only new crops of beans, not more than 3 months old, if possible. Sort the beans, removing and discarding the broken pieces. Wash well. Soak in cold water with a pinch of chlorinated lime for 2 to 3 hours.

To drain, place beans in a plastic bag and follow the same procedure as for sprouting mung beans. In addition, each evening add a pinch of chlorinated lime to about 1 quart soaking water. In about 6 to 7 days the sprouts will be 2 to 3 inches long and ready to eat. Store in the same manner as the mung bean sprouts.

Fa Ya Tou   發芽豆

HOW TO SPROUT AND COOK FAVA BEANS

½ *pound dried fava beans, with seed coats*
2 *teaspoons salt*
2 *whole star anises*
1 *tablespoon corn oil*

Cover the beans with cold water and let them soak at room temperature for 2 days. After 2 days, put the drained beans in a cloth bag. Twist the bag to close, then soak in a bowl of warm water for 2 minutes. Leave the bag of beans to drain and keep the bag and beans in the bowl without the water. Repeat this warm bath twice a day (morning and evening) for 2 days. The beans will gradually sprout. The beans are best tasting if their sprouts are not longer than ½ inch. For a softer texture of dried fava beans, let beans sprout for 4 days.

Preparation and Cooking:
Rinse the beans with sprouts in cold water and place them in a stainless steel saucepan. Add cold water to cover and bring to a boil. Cover and simmer for about 45 minutes or until the beans are very soft. Add the salt, star anise, and oil and cook for 20 minutes more. There will be very little sauce left. Serve warm or cold.

Yield: 3 cups cooked fava bean sprouts. Serve as a side dish, snack, or with cocktails.

Variation: Fava bean sprouts can be deep fried and sprinkled with salt when hot.

4 Wheat Gluten, Eggs, and Seeds and Nuts

NAME OF DISH	NATURE OF DISH	PAGES
Wheat Gluten	Homemade wheat gluten is made from wheat dough and can be fried, boiled, or steamed. This dish supplies protein and is an excellent meat substitute.	99–100
Braised Wheat Gluten with Dried Mushrooms and Bamboo Shoots	Wheat gluten absorbs other flavors easily. This substantial and well-flavored dish can be reheated.	101
Mock Abalone with Fresh Vegetables	In this dish canned seasoned wheat gluten, a handy ingredient, is cooked with fresh vegetables as a one-dish meal.	102–103
Sweet-and-Sour Fried Wheat Gluten	Homemade or ready-made deep-fried wheat gluten balls cooked in a subtle sweet-and-sour sauce.	103–104
Buddha's Delight	A one-dish vegetarian meal consisting of a variety of vegetables with or without fermented bean curd. High in protein.	104–105
Curried Wheat Gluten and Potatoes	A substantial curry flavored, rice-sending dish.	106
Smoked Eggs	Seasoned smoke-flavored soft eggs make an excellent first course dish.	107
Braised Hard-Boiled Eggs	Hard-boiled eggs are scored to absorb the seasoning. This dish, which can be cooked ahead of time, is usually served as an appetizer.	108
Steamed Egg Custard	A smooth salty egg custard which is steamed instead of baked and is very good with plain rice.	108–109

Wheat gluten, a unique processed food, is made by rinsing the starch out of wheat flour dough. Although it is not difficult to make, it is generally considered more sophisticated than most soybean products and, as such, is often used as an ingredient for vegetarian banquet dishes. With its unique texture, flexibility, and high protein value, wheat gluten has become a major meat substitute in vegetarian cooking.

Wheat gluten, whether deep fried, steamed, or boiled, has a soft, flexible texture. Although it has a delicate taste of its own, it readily absorbs flavors and tastes of other foods. Ready-made wheat gluten products may be cooked by themselves or with vegetables. At present, they are available fresh, dried, frozen, and canned, plain or seasoned. Both domestic and imported products are marketed under different names and brands.

For vegetarians who eat eggs, egg dishes play an important role in daily meals. Eggs mix well with most other foods, are highly nutritious, readily available, reasonably priced, and easy to cook. They may be used as the principal ingredient or as supplements. There are two types of Chinese preserved eggs: the renowned thousand-year-old egg is available ready to eat, and can be combined with fresh eggs; salted eggs are hard-boiled and eaten hot or cold.

Historically, the Chinese have done little dairy farming, and consequently traditional Chinese cooking infrequently uses dairy products, such as milk and cheese. Today, however, for the Chinese living in the United States, milk and cheese have become basic food supplements, particularly for the vegetarians who have less access to soybean products. These ingredients are used to prepare cream sauces which may be added to vegetable dishes, thus bringing new flavors to traditional Chinese dishes.

Today, fruits, seeds and nuts are appreciated as healthy, nutritious foods. The Chinese have believed this for many years and, according to a study of vegetarian cooking in early Chinese history, fruits, seeds and nuts have always been important supplements to rice, beans, and vegetables. Originally the Chinese classified fruits and nuts into five major groups: apricots and almonds, peaches, walnuts, chestnuts, and prunes and dates. Of course, there were many others available and some of them, as we see them today, were just as important, including apples, oranges, sesame seeds, watermelon seeds, sunflower seeds, lotus seeds, and ginkgo nuts.

As in the Western world, fruit is usually served fresh in China. In addition, the Chinese often serve dried and preserved fruits as snacks instead of candy or cookies. Not only are they readily available, but they are more substantial and nutritious. Occasionally, fresh and preserved fruits are also used to make desserts, such as spun apples and spun bananas.

Like preserved fruit, seeds and nuts are often served as snacks or with cocktails. In Chinese cooking, they are not considered major ingredients, but they are often used in various dishes to create different tastes and textures. Almonds are a favorite nut because of their texture and flavor. They are eaten as snacks or used in sweets and desserts, such as roasted almonds, almond cream, and almond cookies. Walnuts are also popular among the Chinese people, particularly the vegetarians. They have a taste and texture entirely different from almonds and are used as snacks or to make walnut cream and candy-coated walnuts.

Roasted sesame seeds, sesame oil, and sesame paste are very commonly used as condiments. Sesame seeds are considered one of the most nutritious foods. Sesame oil can be used in cooking but because of its unusual fragrance, it is mostly added as a garnish. Sesame paste is used in making sauces and sometimes serves as a substitute for peanut butter, particularly when used in a sauce for noodles.

Although peanuts actually belong to the legume family, they often are classified as a variety of nut. Because they are more reasonably priced and more readily available in China, peanuts are quite often used as a substitute for other seeds and nuts. They can be cooked in dishes or prepared as snacks by themselves or with other ingredients. Peanuts are also quite often used as an alternative to soybeans. Although they are not as nutritious as soybeans, peanuts have a very pleasing flavor. Some peanut products, however, are comparable to soybean products, such as peanut butter and peanut oil.

Chinese chestnuts, particularly those grown in Liang Hsiang in Northern China, have an unusual flavor and texture. Although they are small, they are sweet and have an unusually smooth texture. When roasted, they make a popular snack. Fresh or dried chestnuts are used for such items as chestnut cake and chestnut candies. In Chinese vegetarian cooking, chestnuts are often cooked with leafy vegetables because of their texture and natural sweet taste.

Red jujube dates are another Chinese specialty and are particularly favored by vegetarians. Despite a relatively thick skin, they have a natural sweet taste and an unusually pleasant fragrance. They can be cooked alone in sweet soups or with other ingredients, such as longan, lotus seeds, or plain congee. When pureed, they can be used as a filling or stuffing for different kinds of sweet rice cakes, such as eight precious pudding or harvest moon cake.

Young lotus seeds can be eaten as a fruit. Two coverings have to be removed, but they taste sweet and tender. Mature ginkgo nuts and lotus seeds have a refreshing and fragrant taste and are used in sophisticated dishes at banquets and New Year festivals, such as Buddha's Delight and lotus seed sweet soup.

Mien Chin   麵筋

WHEAT GLUTEN

    3 *cups flour, preferably high gluten flour*
    1 *teaspoon salt*
    1 *teaspoon dried yeast*
1¼ *cup warm water (approximately)*
    2 *cups peanut or corn oil*

Preparation:
Place the flour in a large mixing bowl. Dissolve the salt and yeast in the warm water, then slowly pour this into the flour while mixing into a firm dough. Knead the dough into a very smooth ball.

(An electric mixer with a dough hook may be used, but only if the recipe is doubled.) Let rest in a covered bowl for at least 4 hours.

Punch down the dough and knead into a ball. Return the dough to the covered bowl and keep in the refrigerator for at least 2 hours.

To remove the starch, wash the dough in a large pot of cold water. Squeeze the dough as if you were rinsing a sponge, so that most of the starch will be removed. (If you wish to save the wheat starch, see the Note below.) To remove any remaining starch from the gluten dough, change the water, and squeeze some more until the water runs clear. (If the gluten becomes separated, add 1 teaspoon salt, combine well, and the dough will stick together again.) The gluten is now ready to be boiled or steamed, or deep fried, then used in various dishes.

Boiling or Steaming: Break the raw gluten into 1-inch chunks and shape into balls. Add to 3 cups cold water. Always bring the water to a boil slowly. Boil the balls for about 5 minutes. If steaming the balls, place gluten balls ½ inch apart on an oiled plate on a steamer rack and steam for 5 minutes.

Deep Frying: In a wok heat the oil to 325°. Break the gluten into 1-inch pieces and shape into balls. Fry the balls on all sides. Keep the gluten balls submerged in the hot oil so that they will puff up in the center. Constantly turn and push them to the side of the pan until they puff up to 2 inches in diameter, about 5 minutes.

Yield: 24 to 26 1½-inch boiled or steamed gluten balls or 2-inch deep-fried gluten balls.

Note: The starch water can be used in recipes calling for wheat starch. Put the starch water in a large pot and let sit for 20 minutes. Slowly pour off ½ to 1 cup of the cleared water. Mix the starch with the remaining water and pour into a muslin bag. Tie the top together and set the bag in the sink on a rack. Place a pot of water on top of the bag to squeeze out the water. Let sit until most of the moisture in the starch is gone. Dry the starch under the sun or in the open air. Use a rolling pin to break it into a fine powder. This resulting powder is wheat starch.

Hung Shao Mien Chin 紅燒麵筋

BRAISED WHEAT GLUTEN WITH DRIED MUSHROOMS
AND BAMBOO SHOOTS

4 *large dried mushrooms, preferably winter mushrooms*
1 *cup warm water*
24 *fried wheat gluten balls, each about 2 inches in diameter,
    homemade (page 99) or ready-made*
2 *tablespoons peanut or corn oil*
1 *cup bamboo shoot slices, each 1 x 2 x ¼-inch*
1½ *teaspoons sugar*
3 *tablespoons soy sauce*
⅛ *teaspoon monosodium glutamate*
1½ *cups carrot slices, each 1 x 2 x ¼-inch*

Preparation:
Wash the mushrooms and soak in warm water for ½ to 1 hour, or
until soft. Drain the mushrooms, but reserve the water. Cut off and
discard the stems, then cut each mushroom cap into quarters.

If ready-made gluten is used, wash with hot water several times to
reduce any strong oil flavor.

Cooking:
Heat a saucepan over medium heat until it becomes hot. Add the
oil and the bamboo shoots, then stir-fry for about 3 to 4 minutes.
Add the mushrooms and stir-fry for another minute. Add the fried
gluten balls, sugar, soy sauce, monosodium glutamate, and mushroom water. Add enough fresh water to make 1 cup. Cover and
bring to a boil, then reduce the heat, simmer for about 10 minutes.
Add the carrots. Cook for 10 minutes more or until the carrots are
tender. Serve hot. The dish can be reheated.

Yield: 4 servings or up to 8 when served with other dishes.

Variations: Other vegetables, such as celery cabbage or bok choy,
may be used instead of carrots.

Su Shih Ching

素 十 景

MOCK ABALONE WITH FRESH VEGETABLES

Chinese canned vegetarian mock abalone or vegetarian mock duck are made from wheat gluten. They are well seasoned, and have the appearance and texture of abalone or duck, but not the taste. As meat substitutes, they have high nutritive values. The Worthington Food Product Company cans vegetable steak and vegetarian scallops* with a texture similar to Chinese gluten balls. These can be used in this dish, but the seasonings must be adjusted.

    2 *carrots, sliced*
    2 *cups water*
   ½ *pound fresh mushrooms, sliced*
   10 *peeled water chestnuts, sliced*
   10 *snow peapods*
    3 *tablespoons peanut or corn oil*
    1 *teaspoon salt*
    1 *10-ounce can vegetarian mock abalone or vegetarian mock duck*
       (Worthington Foods) or 1 recipe Deep-Fried Wheat Gluten
       Balls (page 99)
   ½ *cup water*
    1 *teaspoon cornstarch combined with 2 tablespoons water*

Preparation and Cooking:
Parboil the carrots in the 2 cups water and set aside with the mushrooms, water chestnuts, and snow peapods.

Heat a wok until hot. Add the oil and stir-fry the carrots, mushrooms, water chestnuts, and snow peapods for 2 minutes. Add the salt and stir to mix well. Add the mock abalone, mock duck, or wheat gluten balls, and stir-fry over high heat for another 2 minutes. Add the ½ cup water and bring to a boil. Cover and cook over medium-high heat for 2 minutes. Stir some more to mix. Stir the cornstarch mixture very thoroughly and add to the sauce in the wok, stirring constantly until the sauce thickens. Remove and serve hot.

*Worthington Food Product Company uses the term "skallops" for vegetable scallops.

Yield: 4 servings or up to 8 when served with other dishes.

Note: This dish may be cooked ahead of time, but set the snow peapods aside. Add to the dish and cook long enough to heat through.

T'ang Ts'u Mien Chin

糖醋麵筋

SWEET-AND-SOUR FRIED WHEAT GLUTEN

12 *Deep-Fried Wheat Gluten Balls (page 99) or ready-made*
 1 *cup 1-inch cubes of green pepper or broccoli or any other green vegetable*
 1 *cup julienne strips of carrots*

Sauce:
¼ *cup sherry*
¼ *cup distilled white vinegar*
 2 *tablespoons soy sauce*
 2 *tablespoons catsup*
 2 *tablespoons water*
 5 *tablespoons sugar*
 2 *teaspoons cornstarch*

 2 *cups peanut or corn oil*

Preparation:
Cut the gluten balls into strips ½-inch wide. Set on a plate with the green pepper or broccoli and the carrots.

Combine the sauce ingredients in a bowl and set aside.

Cooking:
Heat the oil in a wok. When the oil is about 375°, fry the gluten strips for 2 minutes or until brown and crisp. Use a strainer to remove the fried gluten. Let drain, then keep hot in the oven.

Fry the vegetables in the oil for about 2 minutes. Remove and drain. Strain the oil.

Reheat the wok and put in about 2 tablespoons of the strained oil (reserve the remaining oil for future use). Blend the sauce ingredients making sure cornstarch is completely blended in and the sugar is dissolved. Stirring constantly, add the sauce to the wok. Cook over high heat until the sauce thickens and is shiny. Add the fried gluten strips to the sauce along with the hot fried vegetables. Stir to coat the ingredients with the sauce. Remove and serve hot.

Yield: 4 servings or up to 8 when served with other dishes.

Lo Han Chai   羅漢齋

BUDDHA'S DELIGHT

Buddha's Delight is one of the most popular vegetarian dishes in China. It usually consists of more than 10 outstanding ingredients, and it varies from region to region. It is usually served as a one-dish meal with rice. It is a favorite dish for many people.

    1 *tablespoon dried hair seaweed*
    1 *teaspoon peanut or corn oil*
    4 *dried mushrooms*
    ¼ *cup dried tree ears*
    2 *ounces cellophane noodles*
    2 *ounces dried soybean milk skin* (erh chu)
    5 *cups hot water*
    ½ *cup sliced carrots*
    ½ *cup sliced bamboo shoots*
    ½ *pound celery cabbage, cut into 2 x 1-inch pieces (about 3 cups)*
    ½ *cup canned mock abalone or canned seasoned vegetable steak*
    30 *fresh or canned ginkgo nuts or 10 cooked chestnuts*
    5 *tablespoons peanut or corn oil*
    1 *teaspoon salt*
    2 *teaspoons sugar*
    ¼ *teaspoon monosodium glutamate*
    2 *tablespoons light soy sauce*
    2 *tablespoons fermented bean curd*
    1 *tablespoon sesame oil*

Preparation:
In 5 separate bowls or cups of hot water, soak the hair seaweed (add the teaspoon of oil to make it easier to separate the strands), mushrooms (use warm water, not hot), tree ears, cellophane noodles, and dried soybean milk skin for 20 minutes or until soft.

Drain the mushrooms, but reserve the water. Cut off and discard the stems, then cut each mushroom cap in half. Set aside the carrots, bamboo shoots, and celery cabbage on a large plate with the mushrooms.

Rinse the tree ears several times after soaking. Drain well. Cut the soaked cellophane noodles into pieces 4 inches long. Rinse and cut the soaked soybean milk skin into 2 x 1-inch pieces. On a large plate, set aside the abalone (if vegetable steak is used instead of mock abalone, cut into 1-inch chunks), gingko nuts, and drained hair seaweed.

Cooking:
Heat a wok over medium heat until very hot. Add 3 tablespoons oil and stir-fry the cabbage, bamboo shoots, carrots, and mushrooms for 2 to 3 minutes. Remove and set aside. Heat 2 more tablespoons oil in the wok over medium heat. Stir-fry the ginkgo nuts, cellophane noodles, tree ears, soybean milk skin, and hair seaweed for 2 minutes. Add the mock abalone and cooked vegetables. Stir, mixing well. Add the salt, sugar, monosodium glutamate, and light soy sauce, along with the reserved mushroom water combined with enough water to make 1½ cups. Mix well, cover, and cook for 20 minutes over medium-low heat. There should be very little sauce remaining.

Add the fermented bean curd and sesame oil to the wok, then mix well. Serve piping hot.

Yield: 6 servings or up to 10 when served with other dishes.

Note: This dish can be cooked ahead of time. Just heat it up before serving, then serve very hot.

Chia Li K'ao Fu Yang Shan Yu

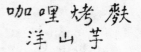

CURRIED WHEAT GLUTEN AND POTATOES

Canned wheat gluten, made by Worthington Foods, is suitable and good in Chinese vegetarian cooking. The following recipe utilizes vegetable scallops.°

    2 *potatoes*
    4 *cups water*
    1 *20-ounce can vegetable scallops (Worthington Foods)*
    2 *tablespoons peanut or corn oil*
    2 *teaspoons imported Madras curry powder*
1½ *teaspoons sugar*

Preparation:
Wash the potatoes and, in a covered pot, cook whole in the water for about 15 minutes. Let cool. Peel off and discard the skins, then cut the potatoes into chunks. You should have about 2 cups.

Drain the vegetable scallops, but reserve the liquid. If large, cut into 1-inch pieces; set aside with the potatoes.

Cooking:
Heat a wok or saucepan over medium heat until hot. Add the oil, curry powder, potatoes, and scallops. Stir-fry for 2 minutes. Add the sugar and reserved liquid. Cook, covered, for about 5 minutes or until the sauce begins to thicken. Serve hot.

Yield: 6 servings or up to 10 when served with other dishes.

°Worthington Food Product Company uses the term "skallops" for vegetable scallops.

Hsün Tan

燻 蛋

SMOKED EGGS

6 *large eggs*
   Cold water

Marinade:
½ *teaspoon salt*
½ *teaspoon sugar*
 2 *tablespoons soy sauce*
 1 *teaspoon sesame oil*
½ *teaspoon liquid smoke (see Note)*

Preparation and Cooking:
Place the eggs in a saucepan and cover with cold water. Place the
pan over medium heat and bring water just to a boil. If the eggs
originally were at room temperature, cook about 4 minutes. If they
were chilled, cook for 5 minutes.

Pour off the water and lightly tap all the eggs with a spoon, just
enough to crack them. Then refill the pan with cold water and add
the eggs. Carefully crack and remove the shells and set aside the
soft-boiled eggs.

In a bowl, combine the salt, sugar, soy sauce, sesame oil, and liquid
smoke, and mix well. Add the eggs and let stand for 1 hour or more.
Turn the eggs a few times to coat evenly. Cut each egg in half
lengthwise and serve chilled. A little marinade may be served with
the eggs.

Yield: 6 servings as an appetizer.

Note: Liquid smoke is available in department stores with gourmet
food shops, and in many supermarkets.

Lu Tan

滷蛋

BRAISED HARD-BOILED EGGS

  6 *large eggs*
     Cold water
  2 *tablespoons peanut or corn oil*
  ½ *cup shredded onion*
  ½ *teaspoon sugar*
  1½ *tablespoons soy sauce*
  1 *tablespoon dry sherry*
  1 *tablespoon water*

Cooking:
Place the eggs in a saucepan, cover with cold water and bring to a
boil. Cover the pan and turn off the flame. Let stand for 20 minutes.
Pour out the hot water.

Crack the shells with the back of a spoon. Refill the pot with cold
water, and add the eggs. Carefully shell the eggs, and set aside.
With a small knife, score each egg lengthwise at ⅛-inch intervals.

Heat a saucepan just large enough to hold the 6 eggs in one layer
on the bottom. Add the oil and stir-fry the onion until brown. Add
the eggs, stir, and add the sugar, soy sauce, sherry, and the tablespoon of water. Cook, covered, for 15 minutes over low heat. Stir
2 to 3 times so that the sauce coats the eggs evenly.

Yield: 6 servings as appetizers or snacks.

蒸蛋

Cheng Tan

STEAMED EGG CUSTARD

  4 *large eggs*
  ½ *teaspoon salt*
  2½ *cups Soybean Sprout Broth (page 130) or ⅛ teaspoon mono-
        sodium glutamate dissolved in 2½ cups water*
  2 *tablespoons chopped canned soy sauce cucumber or homemade
        Soy Sauce Vegetables (page 47)*

Preparation:
In a bowl, beat the eggs until the whites and yolks are well blended.
Stir in the salt. Add the broth, ½ cup at a time, and continue beating lightly until the mixture is well blended but not frothy. Pour
into 4 to 6 rice bowls or cups.

Cooking:
In a pot or skillet large enough to hold the rice bowls or cups, heat
1 quart (or about a depth of 1 inch) water until it is simmering.
Place the bowls or cups in the water. (The water should be halfway
up the sides of the bowls.) Cover the pan tightly and steam for 15
minutes. Sprinkle the chopped Soy Sauce Cucumber on top of the
almost-set egg custards. Cover and continue to steam for 10 more
minutes. Serve hot in the same bowls.

Yield: 4 to 6 servings as a first course.

Variations: Sautéed chopped fresh mushrooms or scallion may be
used instead of Soy Sauce Cucumber, but add ½ teaspoon salt.

Cheng Shuang Tan   蒸 雙 蛋

OLD AND YOUNG STEAMED EGGS

Fresh eggs combined with thousand-year-old eggs create a completely new kind of egg dish. The yolk of a preserved "thousand-
year-old" egg is a greenish grey, and the white is often a brownish
gold color and has a semisolid texture and satiny luster. The yolks
can be separated from the whites and combined with raw fresh
eggs to make a salty custard. The custard is steamed instead of
baked. It is an exotic-looking dish that can be served as an appetizer
for a banquet or dinner party.

 2 *thousand-year-old eggs*
 4 *large fresh eggs*
½ *teaspoon salt*
⅛ *teaspoon monosodium glutamate dissolved in ¼ cup water*

Preparation:
Crack the shells of the thousand-year-old eggs while they are still sealed in their plastic wrappings. Break the wrapper and remove the shell and dried clay. Rinse the shelled eggs under cold water to remove any remaining clay. Separate the white from the yolk. Finely chop the white and dice the yolk. Set aside on separate plates.

Beat the fresh eggs until the whites and yolks are blended. Add the preserved egg yolks, salt, and water containing monosodium glutamate. Beat some more.

Cooking:
Line a soup plate or a small mold with plastic wrap and pour in the egg mixture. Place the plate in a steamer, cover, and steam over low heat for about 20 minutes or until the custard is firmly set.

Let the custard cool, then unmold and cut into 2 x 1 x ¼-inch slices. Arrange slices on a plate. Garnish the center with the preserved egg white. Serve cold.

Yield: 6 servings as an appetizer.

Tan Chiao

OMELETTES WITH CELLOPHANE NOODLES

> 2 *ounces cellophane noodles*
> 2 *cups hot water*
> 4 *large eggs*

Filling:
> 2 *tablespoons peanut or corn oil*
> ½ *cup finely chopped bamboo shoots*
> ½ *cup finely chopped fresh mushrooms*
> 1 *cup finely chopped asparagus, green beans, or other green vege-*
> *table*
> ½ *teaspoon salt*
> 1½ *teaspoons soy sauce*

3 *tablespoons peanut or corn oil*
1 *tablespoon soy sauce*
¼ *teaspoon salt*
⅛ *teaspoon monosodium glutamate combined with* 1 *cup water*

Preparation and Cooking:
Soak the cellophane noodles in hot water for 30 minutes. Cut the soaked noodles into pieces 4 inches long. Drain well and set aside.

Beat the eggs thoroughly and set aside near the cooking area.

Prepare the filling by heating a wok until hot. Add the 2 tablespoons oil, the bamboo shoots, mushrooms, and green vegetable, and stir-fry for about 5 minutes or until the vegetables become quite dry. Add ½ teaspoon salt and 1½ teaspoons soy sauce and mix. Remove and let cool. Add 2 tablespoons of the beaten eggs (take the top foamy part) and combine thoroughly. Set aside.

Heat a 3 to 4-inch ladle or iron skillet until very hot. Turn down the heat to low. Brush on a little oil. Pour in 1 tablespoon beaten egg and swirl to form a pancake 2½ inches in diameter. Put ½ tablespoon of the filling in the center and fold the egg pancake in half, pressing the edge to seal all around before the egg dries. Use a little beaten egg to seal if it is too dry. Remove and set aside on a plate. Repeat the procedure until the beaten eggs and filling mixture are used up. You should have about 16 to 20 small omelettes.

Heat a wok until hot. Add 2 tablespoons of the oil and stir-fry the cellophane noodles. Arrange the omelettes on top of the noodles. Add 1 tablespoon soy sauce, ¼ teaspoon salt, and monosodium glutamate–water mixture. Cover and bring to a boil. Cook over medium heat for 10 minutes. Serve hot.

Yield: 4 servings or up to 8 when served with other dishes.

Note: This dish can be assembled ahead; do not add the monosodium glutamate–water mixture. Keep in the refrigerator uncooked, then cook at the last minute. Then add the water mixture and cook 10 minutes.

Variation: Fresh or frozen peas or any other vegetables may be used instead of cellophane noodles.

Fu Jung Tan

VEGETABLE EGG FU JUNG

     4 *dried mushrooms*
    ⅓ *cup fresh or canned bamboo shoots, cut in julienne strips*
    ½ *cup soaked dried flat-tip bamboo shoots, cut in julienne strips*
     2 *cups fresh bean sprouts, washed and drained*
     1 *scallion, finely shredded*
     5 *tablespoons peanut or corn oil*
     6 *large eggs*
   1½ *teaspoons salt*
    ⅛ *teaspoon white pepper*
    ¼ *teaspoon monosodium glutamate*
    ½ *teaspoon sesame oil*

Preparation:
Wash and soak the dried mushrooms in ½ cup hot water until soft. Drain, remove the stems, and finely shred. Set aside on a plate with the bamboo shoots, flat-tip bamboo shoots, bean sprouts, and scallion.

Heat 2 tablespoons oil in a wok over high heat. Stir-fry the scallion, bean sprouts, both kinds of bamboo shoots, and mushrooms for 2 minutes. Remove and let cool. Beat the eggs thoroughly. Add the vegetable mixture to the beaten eggs, then add salt, pepper, monosodium glutamate, and sesame oil. Mix well with the eggs.

Cooking:
Heat a wok until very hot. Add the remaining 3 tablespoons oil. Before the oil reaches the smoking point, pour in the egg mixture. Using a spatula, push the eggs back and forth, then flip and turn the eggs so that the pieces will be slightly brown on the outside yet soft inside. Serve hot.

Yield: 4 servings for brunch or up to 6 when served with other dishes.

Variations: Stir-fried fresh mushrooms or canned mushrooms may be used instead of dried mushrooms. Shredded celery, carrot or other vegetables may be used instead of dried bamboo shoots.

Tou Sung

豆 鬆

EGGS WITH GREEN BEANS

1   *pound fresh green beans*
2   *large eggs, beaten*
3   *tablespoons peanut or corn oil*
1¼   *teaspoons salt*
½   *teaspoon sugar*
¼   *cup water*

Preparation:
Snap off and discard both ends of the green beans. Wash the beans and drain well. Cut into pea-size pieces. Set aside with the beaten eggs.

Cooking:
Heat a wok until very hot. Add 2 tablespoons of the oil, then the beans. Stir-fry the beans until they turn dark green, about 2 to 3 minutes. Add the salt and sugar, and mix well. Add the water, then cover the wok and cook over high heat for about 3 minutes. By the time the water evaporates, the beans should be cooked but still crisp. Push the beans up the side of the wok. In the center of the wok put the remaining tablespoon of oil and the beaten eggs. Scramble the eggs in the oil until they are cooked to a soft consistency, then combine and cook with the beans. Remove and serve hot.

Yield: 2 servings or up to 6 when served with other dishes.

Variations: Fresh peas or snow peapods may be used instead of green beans.

Yang Ts'ai Pan Tan Szu   洋菜拌蛋絲

AGAR-AGAR SALAD WITH SHREDDED EGG SHEETS

2 *large eggs*
2 *teaspoons dry sherry*
1 *ounce agar-agar*
  Cold water
4 *cups finely shredded lettuce*

Dressing:
1 *tablespoon light soy sauce*
1 *tablespoon distilled white vinegar*
1 *tablespoon sesame oil*
2 *teaspoons sugar*
½ *teaspoon salt*
⅛ *teaspoon monosodium glutamate*

Preparation and Cooking:
Beat the eggs thoroughly with the sherry. Set aside for 30 minutes.
Cut the agar-agar into pieces 1½ inches long. Soak in cold water
for 10 minutes. Drain and squeeze out the water. You should have
about 2 cups. Set the agar-agar in a mixing bowl with the shredded
lettuce and mix well.

Heat an 8-inch skillet until very hot. Reduce the heat to low, and
allow the pan to cool for 1 minute. With a wadded paper towel,
wipe the pan with a little peanut oil. Pour in a fourth of the beaten
eggs and tip the pan around until a thin, round egg sheet forms.
Flip the sheet and cook for 30 seconds more. Transfer to a plate
and let cool. Repeat procedure with the remaining beaten eggs to
make 3 more sheets. Cut the egg sheets, 1 at a time, into pieces 2
inches wide. Stack the strips and cut again into very fine strips 2
inches long. Set aside.

Combine the dressing ingredients. Just before serving, combine the
dressing with the agar-agar–lettuce mixture and transfer onto a
serving platter. Top with the egg strips.

Yield: 2 to 3 servings or up to 6 when served with other dishes.

Variations: Shredded cucumber or white turnips can be used instead of lettuce. Sprinkle with ½ teaspoon salt and let stand for 30 minutes, then squeeze out the excess water.

Liu Li Ke Tan   琉璃鴿蛋

QUAIL EGGS WITH STRAW MUSHROOMS

2 *carrots*
1 *scallion*
1 *8½-ounce can quail eggs (about 30)*
1 *tablespoon soy sauce*
3 *tablespoons peanut or corn oil*
1 *8-ounce can straw mushrooms*
1 *teaspoon salt*
1 *cup chicken broth*
2 *teaspoons cornstarch combined with 2 tablespoons water*

Preparation:
Peel the carrots and roll-cut into 1-inch pieces. You should have about 2 cups. Parboil the carrots for 2 minutes. Rinse in cold water and set aside. Trim and rinse the scallion, then split lengthwise and cut into pieces 2 inches long. Set aside with the carrots on a plate.

Drain and dry the quail eggs. Marinate in the soy sauce for 30 minutes.

Cooking:
Heat a wok until hot. Add the oil and stir-fry the carrots, scallion, and mushrooms with the salt for 2 minutes. Add the chicken broth, cover, and bring to a boil. Add the eggs with the soy sauce and return to a boil. While stirring over high heat, add the well-blended cornstarch mixture. When the sauce thickens and the contents are coated with a clear glaze, remove and serve hot.

Yield: 2 to 3 servings or up to 8 when served with other dishes.

Note: If fresh quail eggs are used, hard boil and shell them, then cook in the same manner.

K'ao Hua Sheng

烤花生

ROASTED PEANUTS

Dry-roasted peanuts have fewer calories than peanuts fried in oil. In roasting, the salt and five-spice powder give the peanuts extra flavor. We often eat these peanuts as snacks or after meals.

1 *pound raw peanuts, with skins (about 3 cups)*
2 *teaspoons fine salt*
1 *teaspoon five-spice powder or 8 pods star anise*

Preparation and Cooking:
Rinse the peanuts in cold water and drain. Put the peanuts on a baking pan just large enough to hold the nuts close together in 1 layer. Add the salt and five-spice powder. Mix well and spread the peanuts close together in 1 layer. Let stand for 10 minutes.

Preheat the oven to 325°. Roast the peanuts in the middle of the oven for 20 minutes. With a spatula, turn the peanuts. Lower the heat to 250° and continue roasting for 1 hour. Let the peanuts cool completely and store in a jar or tin can.

Yield: 3 cups roasted peanuts.

Variation: Skinless peanuts may be used instead.

Hsien Ts'ai Hua Sheng Mi   鹹菜花生米

PEANUTS WITH PRESERVED VEGETABLE

The texture and flavor of the cooked peanuts in the following recipe make it well worth trying. It goes well with congee. This is a typical way of cooking peanuts in my home town, Ningpo.

1 *pound skinless raw peanuts (about 3 cups)*
1 *cup coarsely chopped homemade Salted Red-in-Snow (page 46)*
   or ready-made (Ma-Ling brand)
4 *cups cold water*
1 *to 2 teaspoons salt (depending on the saltiness of the preserved*
   vegetable)

Preparation and Cooking:
Rinse the peanuts several times under cold water. Put them in a saucepan and add the water. Bring to a boil, cover, and lower the heat. Simmer for 45 minutes.

Add the preserved vegetable and salt to the peanuts. Bring to a boil again and continue cooking over low heat for 30 minutes or until the peanuts are soft. Stir twice during this time and watch the liquid; there should be only a small amount of liquid left when the cooking is done. Serve cold.

Yield: 4 cups; serves 8 to 12 as appetizer.

Hua Sheng Mi Pan Tou Fu Kan

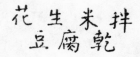

STAR ANISE PEANUTS WITH SEASONED
PRESSED BEAN CURD

The story behind this dish goes as follows: Chin Sheng-tan, a cele-brated literary genius and critic, incurred the royal wrath and was being led to the execution ground to be beheaded. His family fol-lowed the procession in unbearable sadness. But Chin showed very little concern and he bubbled with exquisite wit and humor and composed a couple of very charming poems. Finally, just before he knelt towards the Emperor's Palace, the executioner asked if Chin had any last words for his family. He said he had something to tell his eldest son. The young man, weeping uncontrollably, knelt be-fore his father and strained his ears to listen. "My son," said Chin nonchalantly, "always remember this and pass it on to my grand-children: When you mix roasted peanuts with finely sliced seasoned pressed bean curd dipped in soy sauce and vinegar, it tastes exactly like the famous *chin-hwa* ham." (Smithfield ham is similar to China's *chin-hwa* ham.)

> 2 *3 x 3 x ⅓-inch squares homemade Seasoned Pressed Bean Curd*
> *(page 80) or ready-made*
> ½ *cup homemade Roasted Peanuts (skinless) (page 116) or cocktail*
> *peanuts (if using the latter, adjust seasonings)*

Dressing:
> 1 *tablespoon light soy sauce*
> 1 *teaspoon sugar*
> 2 *teaspoons cider vinegar*
> 1 *tablespoon sesame oil*

Preparation:
Thinly slice or dice the bean curd and combine with the peanuts. Mix the dressing ingredients very well, and toss with the bean curd and peanuts before serving. Serve at room temperature.

Yield: 2 cups; serves 4 to 6 as appetizer.

Variation: Add ½ cup chopped fresh coriander (tender parts of both leaves and stems) to the salad, which will give this dish extra flavor.

T'ai Tiao Hua Sheng Mi

苔 條 花 生 米

PEANUTS WITH SEAWEED

1 *cup peanut or corn oil*
1 *cup raw skinless peanuts*
½ *cup green seaweed* (t'ai tiao)
1 *teaspoon sugar*

Cooking:
Heat a wok until very hot. Add the oil and heat to about 325°. Add the peanuts and fry for about 4 to 5 minutes, stirring to fry evenly. Pour the peanuts and oil into a strainer set over a bowl (reserve leftover oil for future use).

Put 1 tablespoon of the drained oil back into the wok, heat, and stir-fry the seaweed over low heat for 3 to 4 minutes or until crispy. Do not brown. Return the fried peanuts to the wok and mix with the green seaweed, which will stick to the peanuts. Remove, let cool completely, then add the sugar and mix well.

This is a wonderful dish to balance salty dishes and goes well with congee.

Yield: 1½ cups; 4 servings as a side dish.

K'ao Li Tzu

ROASTED CHESTNUTS

烤栗子

1 *pound fresh chestnuts*
   Water

Cooking:
Preheat oven to 325°. Put the chestnuts in a saucepan and cover with water. Brink to a boil and boil for 5 minutes. Drain and spread close together in a single layer on a baking sheet. Bake the chestnuts for about 40 to 60 minutes, depending on their size. Turn off the heat, but keep chestnuts in the oven for 20 minutes.

It is best to serve chestnuts hot. After the chestnuts cool off, just reheat in a 375° oven for 5 minutes.

Note: Roasted chestnuts make an excellent snack in the fall, when fresh chestnuts are plentiful.

5 Soups and Condiments

Traditionally, the Chinese eat their meals without serving a beverage, so large bowls of soup are always welcome. At banquets, soups are served between courses for a change of pace, but ordinarily, they are served simultaneously with the other dishes. Soups can be very light and plain or very elaborate, consisting of many different ingredients. Some soups are quite substantial and heavy, and may serve as the main dish.

In vegetarian cooking, soups often consist of one fresh vegetable or a preserved vegetable or a combination of both. In simple and light soups with few ingredients, such as Fresh Mushroom and Vegetable Soup, Tri-Shredded Soup, and Egg Drop Soup, it is the flavor of the stock that counts. In heavy soups, the flavor derives from the combination of vegetables—fresh vegetables or fresh and preserved vegetables with soybean products. Preserved vegetables create many interesting and appetizing flavors and tastes, such as in Vegetarian Hot-and-Sour Soup, Fava Bean with Preserved Vegetable Soup, or Wheat Gluten with Cellophane Noodles Soup. In addition to a wide variety of ingredients, some heavy soups use thickening agents, such as cornstarch.

To make soups tasier and heartier, whether light or heavy, soybean sprouts and soybeans or mushrooms and bamboo shoots are often used to make the soup bases. These vegetables are stir-fried with oil before water is added to make the stock or soup base. For a quick and simple soup and soup base, soy sauce or salt can be combined and cooked with monosodium glutamate and water. See Soy Sauce Soup.

In Chinese cooking, vegetarians also use various condiments for cooking and for dipping. Some of these are commercially prepared while others may be made in the home according to one's own taste. They add flavor and zest to a dish, and stimulate the appetite.

Chinese salad dressings are made of soy sauce, sesame oil or paste, vinegar, sugar, and hot pepper powder or oil. Soy sauces of different strengths are now widely available and Westerners are learning how to use them. Sesame oil and sesame paste are not as commonly used in salad dressings, because the Chinese use toasted sesame seeds, which have a rather strong flavor. If one finds the flavor of sesame oil disagreeable, one may use another kind of vegetable oil as a substitute, peanut oil, for example, and peanut butter may be substituted for sesame paste. The Chinese use sugar to balance the sourness of vinegar. Hot pepper oil may be added to enhance all the other flavors.

Many different combinations of salad dressings and sauces are used throughout this book with vegetable, soybean, wheat gluten, and rice dishes. They may be used with other salads and dishes, according to your own tastes.

Following are several easy-to-prepare soups that go well with daily meals:

Chiang Yu T'ang   醬 油 湯

SOY SAUCE SOUP

   2 *teaspoon soy sauce*
   1 *teaspoon sesame oil*
   ½ *teaspoon minced scallion*
       Pinch monosodium glutamate
   1 *cup boiling water*

To a large soup bowl add the soy sauce, sesame oil, minced scallion, and monosodium glutamate. Pour in the boiling water.

This is a simple, basic soup to which any kind of cooked ingredients may be added, including cooked won tons or cooked chopped or shredded vegetables.

Yield: 1 serving.

Tan Hua T'ang

蛋花湯

VEGETARIAN EGG DROP SOUP

3 *cups water*
1 *teaspoon peanut or corn oil*
¼ *teaspoon monosodium glutamate*
1 *teaspoon salt*
1 *large egg*
1 *teaspoon finely chopped scallion (optional)*
2 *teaspoons sesame oil*

To a saucepan add the water, peanut or corn oil, monosodium glutamate, and salt, and bring to a boil. Beat the egg thoroughly and pour into the soup very slowly, while gently stirring the soup. Remove the pot from the heat and garnish with the chopped scallion and sesame oil. Serve hot.

Yield: 4 servings.

Variations: To make Seaweed Egg Drop Soup, tear 1 or 2 sheets of laver seaweed into pieces 2 inches square and add to the soup along with the scallion and sesame oil. To make Tomato Egg Drop Soup, parboil 1 medium tomato for 10 seconds, then peel, cut into 8 wedges, and remove the seeds. After you bring the water to a boil, add the tomato and simmer for 5 minutes before adding the beaten egg. Any version of egg drop soup may be thickened with 1½ tablespoons cornstarch combined with ¼ cup cold water.

Su Mi T'ang

粟米湯

CREAM OF CORN SOUP

1 8-ounce can cream of corn
½ 10-ounce package frozen peas and carrots
2 cups water
   Pinch of monosodium glutamate
   Salt to taste

Preparation and Cooking:
Combine above ingredients in a saucepan and cook for 10 minutes.
Serve hot.

Yield: 4 servings.

Note: When the vegetables are in season, this soup can be made
with fresh corn, peas, and carrots.

Variations: For a velvety texture, add 2 lightly beaten egg whites
before serving.

Hsien Ts'ai Tou Pan T'ang

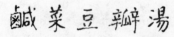

FAVA BEAN WITH PRESERVED RED-IN-SNOW SOUP

1 cup soaked dried fava beans
3 cups water
½ cup finely chopped homemade Salted Red-in-Snow (page 46)
   or ready-made
   Salt to taste
   Pinch of monosodium glutamate
1 teaspoon peanut or corn oil

Preparation and Cooking:
See Puree of Fava Beans (page 90) for soaking the dried fava
beans. Simmer the soaked fava beans in 3 cups water for about 30
minutes or until the beans are very soft but still maintain their
shape. Add the preserved red-in-snow, salt, monosodium glutamate
and oil. Mix well and serve hot.

Yield: 4 servings when served with other dishes.

Ch'ing Ts'ai Ma Ku T'ang   青菜蔴菇湯

FRESH MUSHROOM AND CABBAGE SOUP

1 *tablespoon peanut or corn oil*
1 *cup sliced fresh mushrooms*
2 *cups bok choy or other Chinese green cabbage, cut in 1-inch chunks*
3 *cups water*
  Salt to taste

Preparation and Cooking:
Heat a cook-and-serve pot until hot. Add the oil and mushrooms and stir-fry until the mushrooms begin to soften. Add the bok choy and stir-fry for 2 more minutes. Add the water and bring to a boil. Cook uncovered for 2 to 3 minutes or until the bok choy is soft. Add salt and serve hot.

Yield: 4 servings when served with other dishes.

Variations: Mustard greens, watercress, or lettuce may be used instead of bok choy. Soaked dried mushrooms may be used instead of fresh ones. Luffa may be used instead of bok choy, but remove the hard part of the skin and cut it up into chunks. Cooking is the same. In early spring the young shoots of *Lycium chinense* are good for stir-frying and the leaves and dried seeds can be used in soups. For a substantial one-dish meal, add 10 to 20 pieces of fried wheat gluten to the soup and adjust the seasoning, or add 2 ounces of soaked cellophane noodles in addition to the fried wheat gluten, and this dish becomes Wheat Gluten with Cellophane Noodle Soup.

P'ien Chien Tung Ku T'ang   扁夫冬菇湯

WINTER MUSHROOM WITH FLAT-TIP BAMBOO SHOOTS SOUP

12 *large dried winter mushrooms*
½ *cup dried flat-tip bamboo shoots*
 3 *cups warm water*
 2 *teaspoons peanut or corn oil*

Preparation:
Wash the mushrooms and bamboo shoots and soak in separate bowls, each in 1½ cups warm water, for 1 hour or until soft.

Squeeze out the mushrooms and bamboo shoots, reserving the liquids. Remove and discard the tough stems of the mushrooms, keeping the caps intact. Use your fingers to pull at the larger end of each bamboo shoot and split the shoot into two long strips; then cut into pieces 2 inches long. Set the vegetables aside.

Line a strainer with a paper towel. Strain the mushroom soaking liquid into a bowl large enough to hold 5 to 6 cups of liquid. Add enough water to the mushroom liquid to make 3 cups. Add the trimmed mushroom caps and peanut oil to the mushroom liquid and set aside. Strain the liquid from the soaking bamboo shoots and add it and the cut-up bamboo shoots to another bowl and set aside.

Cooking:
Place a cake rack on the bottom of a deep pot that is large enough to hold the bowl of mushroom liquid and caps. Add enough water so that it reaches up to half the height of the bowl. Cover and bring to a boil. Reduce heat to medium-low and let cook for 1½ hours. Add the reserved bamboo shoots and bamboo shoot soaking liquid, and continue cooking for 30 minutes. Do not let the water in the pot evaporate; add more boiling water, if necessary.

No seasoning is needed because the dried bamboo shoots already contain salt. Serve hot with a meal or at the end. You may strain the soup and use it as broth or sauce base.

Yield: 6 to 8 servings with other dishes.

Note: The dish can be cooked in a Yunnan pot.

Variation: Dried mouth mushrooms may be used instead of winter mushrooms. Since mouth mushrooms are dried without having been washed, there is a lot of sand and mud at the end of the stem. After the mushrooms have soaked, they have to be cleaned thoroughly before being cooked. Allow the sand and mud in the mushroom soaking water to settle. Pour out the clear liquid and discard the sediment. The dark brown liquid from the mushroom soaking water makes a delicious vegetarian soup stock.

Hsien Ts'ai Yang Shan Yu T'ang   鹹菜洋山芋湯
POTATO WITH PRESERVED RED-IN-SNOW SOUP

  1 *medium potato*
  1 *tablespoon peanut or corn oil*
  ½ *cup chopped homemade Salted Red-in-Snow (page 46) or
     ready-made*
  4 *cups water*
    Salt to taste
    Pinch of monosodium glutamate

Preparation and Cooking:
Peel and thinly slice the potato, then cut again into very fine julienne strips not more than 1½ inches long.

Heat the oil in a pot and stir-fry the potato and preserved red-in-snow or vegetables for 2 minutes. Add the water and bring to a boil. Cook for about 10 minutes. Add the salt and monosodium glutamate. Serve hot.

Yield: 6 servings when served with other dishes.

Variations: Add about 2 tablespoons carrots cut in very fine julienne strips and cook with the potato. This adds color as well as texture. Finely shredded *Szechuan cha ts'ai* (¼ cup) may be used instead of preserved red-in-snow.

Huang Tou Ya T'ang

黄 豆 芽 湯

SOYBEAN SPROUT SOUP

1 *pound fresh soybean sprouts*
1 *cup soaked dried soybeans or fava beans (optional)*
3 *tablespoons peanut or corn oil*
4 *cups water*
1 *teaspoon salt*
¼ *teaspoon sugar*
1 *tablespoon light soy sauce*

Preparation:
Pick off and discard the root of each soybean sprout. Rinse under cold water, drain, and set aside. Set aside the soaked beans and the sprouts.

Cooking:
Heat a saucepan and add the oil. Stir-fry the bean sprouts for 3 to 4 minutes. Add the beans and continue to stir-fry a few minutes. Add 4 cups water, cover, and bring to a boil, then simmer for 1 hour or until the beans are very soft. Add the salt, sugar, and soy sauce. Serve hot. The soup can be cooked ahead of time and reheated.

Yield: 6 servings when served with a meal.

Note: A pinch of monosodium glutamate may be added before serving.

Variation: Cut-up peeled potatoes may be used instead of dried beans. To make Soybean Sprout Broth, strain the soup. This broth may also be used as a sauce base.

Po Ts'ai Tou Fu Keng

菠 菜 豆 腐 羹

SPINACH WITH BEAN CURD SOUP

1 *pound fresh spinach*
3 *tablespoons peanut or corn oil*
1 *teaspoon salt*
¾ *teaspoon sugar*
1 *4 x 4 x 1½-inch square fresh tender bean curd, cut up*
3 *cups water*
2 *tablespoons cornstarch combined with ¼ cup cold water*
  Sesame oil
  Salt to taste

Cut the spinach leaves, if too large, into pieces 2 inches long. Wash and drain thoroughly.

Heat a large wok until very hot, then add the peanut oil. Taking as much spinach as you can hold in both hands, cover the hot oil surface of the wok so that the oil does not spatter. Stir until the spinach is slightly wilted and then add the rest. Stir-fry until all of the spinach is wilted. Add the salt and sugar and stir to mix well. Use chopsticks or a fork to remove the spinach from the wok and place in a saucepan (discard the liquid in the wok). Add the spinach, bean curd, and water to the saucepan and bring to a boil. Mix the cornstarch and cold water, add, stirring well until soup thickens. Add a few drops sesame oil and salt to taste before serving.

Yield: 6 servings.

Note: Fresh spinach, when sold loose by weight, is left uncut with roots intact. The stem of the leaf, which is attached to the plant, is pink. This pink part of the stem is sweet and has a good flavor. When the loose fresh spinach is cooked, it tastes far better than the prewashed spinach packed in cellophane bags. The pink stems of the spinach should be cut into 2-inch long pieces along with the leaves and split into 2 to 4 stalks for easy washing and serving.

Variations: Chinese leeks, chrysanthemum greens, and amaranth can be used instead of spinach. Also frozen spinach may be used instead of fresh spinach.

Pai Mu Erh Keng

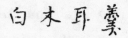

SILVER EARS SOUP

  1 *cup silver ears*
  4 *cups warm water*
  6 *dried mushrooms*
  ½ *cup finely shredded fresh mushrooms*
  2 *cups fresh mung bean sprouts, roots and heads removed*
  ½ *cup finely shredded snow peapods*
  2 *tablespoons peanut or corn oil*
  3 *cups Soybean Sprout Broth (page 130)*
    Salt and white pepper to taste
1½ *tablespoons cornstarch*
  2 *teaspoons sesame oil*

Preparation:
Combine the silver ears with 3 cups of the warm water in a sauce-pan. Slowly bring to a boil and cook, covered, over low heat for 3 to 4 hours, or until they are just soft but not crunchy. With a spoon, break them into small pieces and set aside.

Wash the dried mushrooms and soak in the remaining cup of warm water for 30 minutes. Drain, reserving ½ cup of the mushroom water. Combine the cornstarch with this reserved liquid and set aside. Remove and discard the mushroom stems, then finely shred the caps. Set aside with the fresh mushrooms, bean sprouts, and snow peapods.

Cooking:
Heat a saucepan until hot, add the peanut or corn oil, bean sprouts, and soaked dried mushrooms and stir-fry for 2 minutes. Add the Soybean Sprout Broth, bring to a boil and add the fresh mushrooms, silver ears, and snow peapods. Bring to a boil again and add the salt and pepper. Stir the cornstarch mixture until well combined and slowly pour it into the soup, stirring until it boils again. The soup will thicken slightly. Pour into a tureen or individual bowls. Garnish with drops of sesame oil.

Yield: 6 servings as a first course.

San Szu T'ang

三 絲 湯

TRI-SHREDDED SOUP

 6 *dried mushrooms*
   Warm water
½ *cup finely shredded winter bamboo shoots*
½ *recipe Shredded Egg Sheets (page 114)*
 1 *tablespoon peanut or corn oil*
¼ *teaspoon monosodium glutamate*
 1 *teaspoon salt or to taste*
 1 *teaspoon sesame oil*

Preparation:
Wash the mushrooms and soak in warm water for 30 minutes. Drain, but reserve the soaking water. Add enough water to make 3 cups liquid. Set aside. Cut off and discard the mushroom stems. Cut the caps into shreds. Set aside the mushrooms with the bamboo shoots and the Shredded Egg Sheets on a large plate.

Cooking:
Heat a saucepan over medium heat until hot. Add the peanut or corn oil, bamboo shoots and mushrooms. Stir-fry for 2 minutes but do not let them brown. Add the reserved 3 cups water, Shredded Egg Sheets, monosodium glutamate, salt, and sesame oil. Serve hot.

Yield: 6 servings.

Note: For a tastier soup use Soybean Sprout Broth (page 130) instead of the water.

Kuo Pa T'ang   鍋巴湯
VEGETARIAN SIZZLING RICE SOUP

4 *4 x 4-inch Fried Rice Patties (page 150)*
1 *recipe Tri-Shredded Soup (page 133)*

Cooking:
Preheat oven to 475°. Set the Rice Patties on a heatproof plate.
Just before serving, heat in the hot oven for about 7 to 8 minutes.

In a cook-and-serve pot bring the Tri-Shredded Soup to a boil. Take
the hot soup and hot Rice Patties to the dinner table. Add the Rice
Patties to the soup. If the Rice Patties and soup are hot, they will
sizzle.

Yield: 6 servings as a first course.

Note: Any kind of soup may be combined with Rice Patties, as long
as they are both hot and combined at serving time.

Su Ts'ai T'ang   素菜湯
VEGETABLE SOUP

  4 *cups diced cabbage (½-inch cubes)*
  1 *cup diced carrots*
  1 *cup diced potato*
  ½ *cup diced seeded green pepper*
  1 *medium yellow onion, diced*
  1 *large tomato, parboiled, skinned, seeded, and diced*
  5 *tablespoons peanut or corn oil*
  7 *to 8 cups water*
1½ *teaspoons salt or to taste*

Preparation and Cooking:
Set aside the vegetables on two large plates.

Heat a large saucepan. Stir-fry the green pepper with 1 tablespoon
of the oil until soft. Remove and set aside.

Heat the remaining oil in the same pan and stir-fry the onion until it becomes translucent. Add the cabbage, carrots, and potatoes and stir-fry 3 to 4 minutes or until they are soft and dry. Add the tomatoes, and stir some more. Add 6 cups of the water and bring to a boil. Partly cover and let cook over medium heat for 2 hours. Maintain the water level by adding more boiling water when needed. Add the salt, and cooked pepper. Serve hot.

Yield: 8 servings when served with a meal.

Variations: For Vegetable Broth, strain the soup; the sizes of the chopped vegetables would not be important. Any vegetables can be added, such as celery, fresh mushrooms, or zucchini, as long as they are first separately stir-fried with oil then combined to cook together.

Suan La T'ang   酸 辣 湯

VEGETARIAN HOT-AND-SOUR SOUP

30 *day lily buds*
 2 *tablespoons dried tree ears*
 1 *4 x 4 x 1½-inch piece fresh tender bean curd*
 ¾ *teaspoon salt*
 3 *cups strained Soybean Sprout Broth (page 130), Vegetable Broth
     (above), or Soy Sauce Soup (page 124)*
 1 *tablespoon soy sauce*
 ¼ *teaspoon white pepper*
 2 *tablespoons cider vinegar*
1½ *tablespoons cornstarch combined with ¼ cup water*
 1 *egg*
 1 *teaspoon sesame oil*
 2 *teaspoons minced scallion*

Preparation:
Soak the day lily buds and tree ears in hot water in separate bowls for 30 minutes or until soft. Pick off and discard the hard ends, if any, of the lily buds. Pile the buds together, then cut in half. Wash the tree ears several times, drain, squeeze dry, and break into small pieces. You should have about 1 cup. Set aside with the lily buds.

Handle the bean curd gently. Slice it ¼ inch thick, then cut again into 2-inch-long julienne strips. Sprinkle with ¼ teaspoon of the salt and set aside for 10 minutes.

In a 2-quart saucepan, combine the soup stock, ½ teaspoon salt, the soy sauce, lily buds, and tree ears. Drop the bean curd into the stock. Add the white pepper and vinegar. Up to this point the soup can be prepared in advance and stand a few hours.

Cooking:
Cover the pan and slowly bring the soup to a boil. Blend the cornstarch with the water and slowly pour into the soup, stirring gently until it thickens and boils again. In a bowl beat the egg thoroughly. Remove the soup from the heat and slowly pour in the beaten egg. Let it stand for a few seconds to allow the hot soup to cook the egg. Stir in the sesame oil and sprinkle the top with the scallion. Serve at once.

Yield: 6 to 8 servings as a first course.

Variations: For those who dislike a hot, peppery soup, omit the vinegar and pepper; this soup then becomes Mandarin Soup. Stir-fried fresh mushrooms and cabbage may be used instead of lily buds and tree ears.

Following are two kinds of hot pepper sauces for cooking or for serving with a meal as a relish. They will certainly increase your appetite.

Canton La Chiao Chiang　　　廣東辣椒醬

CANTONESE HOT PEPPER BEAN SAUCE

⅓ *cup corn oil*
2 *cloves garlic, finely minced*
5 to 10 *dried hot peppers, to taste, coarsely chopped*
5 to 10 *fresh hot peppers, depending on the size, coarsely chopped*
　　　(about 1½ cups)
¼ *cup salted black beans*
2 *tablespoons brown bean sauce*
2 *teaspoons sugar*

Preparation and Cooking:
Heat a wok until very hot. Add the oil, garlic, and dried and fresh peppers, and stir-fry for about 2 minutes. Add the salted black beans to the garlic and peppers and cook together over low heat for 5 minutes or until the peppers are wilted. Add the brown bean sauce and sugar and cook a few minutes. Let the sauce cool completely. When cold, transfer to a jar and keep in the refrigerator.

Yield: 1 cup.

Note: Adding dried hot peppers will increase the hot flavor, but you may omit them if the fresh hot peppers are hot enough.

Szechuan Tou Pan Chiang　　　四川豆瓣醬

SZECHUAN HOT PEPPER BEAN SAUCE

20 *2-inch long dried hot peppers*
½ *cup water*
1 *pound fresh sweet peppers, preferably the red*
6 *tablespoons corn oil*
2 *cloves garlic, finely minced*
¼ *cup brown bean sauce (whole or ground)*

Preparation:
Soak the dried hot peppers in the water until they are very soft. Drain, reserving the soaking water, and finely chop the pepper.

Wash the sweet peppers. Drain and dry thoroughly. Cut and discard the seeds and pith. Coarsely chop the sweet peppers and set aside.

Cooking:
Heat the oil in a heavy saucepan with an asbestos pad on the burner. Add the chopped hot peppers and the garlic, and stir and cook in the oil for 2 minutes. Add the bean sauce, sweet peppers, and the soaking water. Bring to a boil and cook together, uncovered, over low heat for about 30 minutes or until the liquid has evaporated, stirring often during this time.

Let cool completely. Keep sauce submerged under the red-hot oil and in a jar with a tight cover at room temperature for weeks, or in the refrigerator indefinitely.

Yield: 1 cup.

Note: The degree of hotness will vary according to the amount of dried hot peppers added to the sauce; therefore, the proportions of hot and sweet peppers are adjustable according to one's personal taste.

Hua Chiao Yen   花 椒 鹽

ROASTED SALT AND SZECHUAN PEPPERCORNS

½ *cup coarse salt*
 2 *tablespoons Szechuan peppercorns*
 1 *teaspoon whole black peppercorns*

Preparation and Cooking:
Combine and heat the ingredients in a dry pan. Stir the spices or shake the pan a few times while roasting until the peppercorns are fragrant, about 5 minutes. Cool, then crush with a rolling pin or in a blender.

Strain through a fine sieve. Use the mixture sparingly as a dip for dishes that call for it. Store the seasoning in a covered jar.

Yield: Approximately ¼ cup.

La Yu　　　　　　　　　　　　　　　辣油

HOT PEPPER OIL

½ *cup corn oil*
2 *tablespoons cayenne pepper*
1 *teaspoon paprika*

Preparation and Cooking:
Heat the oil in a wok until it just starts to smoke. Turn off the heat, wait for 30 seconds (if using a heavy pan, wait a little longer), then add the cayenne pepper and paprika. Stir well and let sit until the solids settle. Strain the oil through a paper towel-lined strainer. Discard the solids. The oil can be kept in a jar without refrigeration. Use 1 to 2 teaspoons for a dish or as a dip according to taste.

Yield: Approximately ½ cup.

Chiang Chiang Szu　　　　　　　醬薑絲

SOY SAUCE MARINATED GINGERROOT

You may use any amount of fresh gingerroot (preferably young) that you wish. Soy Sauce Marinated Gingerroot will keep in the refrigerator for months.

Preparation:
Wash and dry the gingerroot thoroughly. With a paring knife, scrape off the skin. *Wipe clean and dry each piece.* Cut each piece into paper-thin slices, then cut again into the finest strips not more than 1½ inches long. Put them in a clean jar. Pour in light soy sauce to cover the ginger strips. Cover tightly and keep in the refrigerator. The ginger is always ready for any dish that calls for ginger. The marinating soy sauce can also be used in dishes that call for soy sauce.

6 Rice, Noodles, Buns, Dumplings, and Tien Hsin

NAME OF DISH	NATURE OF DISH	PAGES
Boiled Rice	Plain boiled rice—only rice and water are used. This can be kept warm in the oven and easily reheated.	145
Steamed Rice	An excellent method for cooking rice. Convenient for servings of 2 or less.	146
Baked Rice	Another method of cooking plain rice. Leftover baked rice can be reheated.	146
Egg Fried Rice	Fried rice can be made of leftover rice that has been boiled, steamed, or baked. Cooked vegetables may be added for variations.	147
Vegetable Rice	Plain boiled rice is combined with stir-fried cabbage and lightly seasoned with salt. Beans and peas can be used as variations.	147–148
Plain Rice Congee	Congee is a thick rice soup which can be served hot with small highly seasoned dishes, leftovers, or simply served plain with sugar to taste. It is very soothing.	148–149
Vegetable Rice Congee	Plain rice congee is combined with cabbage and seasoned with salt. This can be eaten with side dishes of seasoned beans or peanuts.	149
Rice Patties	A basic recipe for fried rice patties and sizzling rice patty dishes.	150
Two-sides Browned Noodles	Egg noodle patty is browned until crispy on both sides and topped with vegetables and gravy.	151–152

For thousands of years, the Chinese have eaten rice or other grains as their staple food. Polished white rice has a smooth and easy-to-eat texture. However, it is less nutritious than brown rice. For those who are not used to eating brown rice, it is suggested that a portion of brown rice be mixed with white rice.

There are three types of rice: long-grain, oval-grain, and glutinous or sweet rice. The latter is usually used for stuffings and sweet *tien hsin*, while long-grain and oval-grain rice are served plain. Long and oval grains offer different textures, and the choice is a matter of personal preference.

In China, plain rice is boiled or steamed. Perhaps the easiest and most convenient way to cook plain rice is to use an automatic electric rice cooker. In the United States, plain rice also is baked in the oven. White or brown rice also can be prepared with vegetables, beans, or sweet potatoes. After plain rice is cooked, it can be combined with eggs or other ingredients to make egg-fried rice.

Glutinous rice can be cooked sweet or salty to serve different purposes. For example, it is used in eight precious pudding and Steamed Dumplings *(Shao Mai)*.

Rice Patties are baked in the oven and then deep fried. These are fragrant and crispy, and have a flavor of their own. They can be served hot or cold, and can be reserved and reheated in the oven for many interesting uses. For example, they can be served as a snack by adding a little bit of salt; they can be added to soup stock to make a sizzling soup; and they can be used as a base for any dish with a gravy. Rice Patties add a lot of texture and body to any dish.

Congee, an easily digestible porridge, is made with rice. This dish serves several different purposes: not only is it tasty, but it also is soothing to the sick and to those who have overeaten. In most parts of China, congee is usually made from plain rice and water for breakfast. The thickness of the congee can be adjusted according to one's taste. It must be served very hot and, at meals other than breakfast, is usually accompanied by cold side dishes, such as fresh or preserved eggs, vegetables, soybeans, soybean products, peanuts, or leftover dishes.

For the vegetarian, congee can also be cooked with vegetables or soybeans, mung beans, or red beans and can be served plain, salted, or sweetened. Vegetable Rice Congee can be seasoned with salt, while bean congee can be seasoned with sugar.

Many kinds of noodles come in various forms and textures for different uses. They are easy to cook and are usually topped with fresh or preserved vegetables, such as bamboo shoots or mushrooms. They can also be fried, cooked in soups, boiled and served plain with a hot or cold sauce.

In Central and Southern China, people also eat noodles made from rice. These are cooked by similar methods. The Chinese consider noodles a symbol of longevity. Thus, noodle dishes are always served at birthday parties in place of the birthday cakes found in Western cultures. In Northern China, wheat is more readily available than rice; consequently, noodles and buns made of wheat flour are eaten as rice substitutes. Plain noodles and buns are eaten together with other foods, such as vegetables and bean products. For Chinese vegetarians, buns are often stuffed with different kinds of vegetables and bean products. Or, wheat flour can be made into dough for stuffed dumplings *(chiao tzu),* in a variety of forms and tastes.

In provinces outside of Northern China, noodles and buns are treated as *tien hsin,* meaning "to dot your heart." *Tien hsin,* just like cakes or pastries, are eaten as snacks between meals. They are usually less doughy and are filled with stuffing to provide different tastes. Although they are less substantial than regular meals, they are just as tasty. *Tien hsin* are quite often eaten as a light lunch or even a light supper, and fancy ones are made for banquets.

Some *tien hsin* made from wheat flour and other grain flour doughs are sweet rather than salty and are served as desserts. Examples include Fried Custard, Date Wontons, Red Bean Paste Buns, and steamed rice cakes. In some regions, sweet *tien hsin* are cooked in soups such as Almond Cream, silver ears or lily buds sweet soup, and peanut soup.

Pai Fan   白飯

PLAIN RICE

The following are different methods of cooking plain Chinese rice. Only water and rice are used. The proportions of rice and water vary, depending on the dryness of the rice, and personal tastes.

Chu Fan   煮飯

BOILED RICE

Long-grain rice: With 1 cup rice, use 1¾ cups water; with 2 cups rice, use 3 cups water; and with 3 cups rice, use 4 cups water. Thereafter, use an additional ⅞ cup water for each cup rice. (1 cup raw rice yields 3 cups cooked rice.)

Oval-grain rice: With 1 cup rice, use 1½ cups water; with 2 cups rice, use 2½ cups water. Thereafter, use an additional ⅞ cup water for each cup rice. (1 cup raw rice yields 2½ cups cooked rice.)

Preparation and Cooking:
Wash and drain the rice several times. To a heavy saucepan with a tightly fitting lid, add the washed rice and the correct proportion of fresh water. Place the saucepan over medium heat and bring the rice to a boil. Boil for 3 to 4 minutes or until all the water appears to be absorbed by the rice. Cover with the lid and turn heat down to a low simmer. Cook for 20 minutes. Turn off the heat but do not remove the pot from the stove or lift the cover; let the rice steam for 10 minutes.

Fluff the rice with wet chopsticks. Serve in warm bowls. Rice can be kept hot in a covered casserole in the oven at 140° to 170° for up to 30 minutes without drying out.

Cheng Fan

蒸飯

STEAMED RICE

2 *cups oval- or long-grain rice*
  Water: 2 cups for oval-grain rice, 2½ cups for long-grain rice

Preparation and Cooking:
Wash and drain the rice several times. Put the washed rice in a large heatproof bowl and add the water. Let the rice soak in the water for 30 minutes.

Place the bowl with rice and water on a rack in a pot containing several inches of water. The water level should reach about 1½ inches below the bowl's rim. Cover the pot or wok. Bring the water to a boil and steam the rice over medium heat for about 30 minutes or until soft. Fluff the rice with wet chopsticks and serve in the same bowl. If the bowl has a cover, cover the rice between servings.

K'ao Fan

烤飯

BAKED RICE

  2 *cups long-grain rice*
2½ *cups water*

Preparation:
Wash the long-grain rice several times and drain. To an oven-proof container with a cover, add the washed rice and the fresh water. Let the rice soak in the water for 30 minutes, and do not drain.

Cooking:
Preheat the oven to 350°. Cover the rice (and the soaking water) and bake for 40 minutes. Reduce the heat to 200° and continue baking for 10 more minutes. Serve hot in the same baking container.

Leftover Boiled, Steamed, or Baked Rice can be heated in the steamer, or you can add a little water to the rice, bring to a boil, then cook over low heat for 10 to 15 minutes. It is also excellent to use for fried rice with or without an egg.

Tan Ch'ao Fan

蛋炒飯

EGG FRIED RICE

3 *tablespoons peanut or corn oil*
2 *tablespoons chopped scallion*
3 *cups leftover cooked rice*
1 *large egg*
  Salt to taste

Preparation and Cooking:
Heat a wok or pan until very hot. Add 2 tablespoons of the oil and
the chopped scallion and stir-fry for a few seconds, then add the
cooked rice (separate the grains when rice is cold). Stir-fry until
the rice is hot, about 2 minutes. Push the rice to the side, making a
well in the center. Add the remaining 1 tablespoon oil. Break the
egg into the center and scramble it with the oil until it has a soft
consistency, then mix it into the rice. Add the salt and mix well.
Serve hot.

Yield: 2 servings.

Variations: Cooked vegetables, such as green beans, peas, snow
peapods, vegetable steaks, chopped lettuce, and chopped spinach
may be added to the rice. Add salt and monosodium glutamate to
taste.

Ts'ai Fan

VEGETABLE RICE

1 *pound bok choy or other Chinese cabbage*
3 *tablespoons peanut or corn oil*
1½ *teaspoons salt*
2 *cups long-grain rice, washed and drained*
3 *cups water*

Preparation and Cooking:
Wash and drain the bok choy. Cut the stalk and leaves into ½-inch
pieces. Set aside.

Heat a wok or pot until very hot. Add the oil and bok choy and stir-fry for 2 to 3 minutes. Add the salt, mix well, and remove from heat.

Follow the recipe for Boiled Rice. Combine the cleaned rice with the 3 cups water. After the rice boils for 3 to 4 minutes and the water is absorbed, add the partially cooked bok choy and pan juices, and mix in with the rice. Cover and reduce heat to a low simmer. Cook for 30 minutes. Turn off the heat and let the rice stand for 10 minutes without raising the cover. Serve hot with other dishes.

Yield: 6 servings.

Variation: To make Bean or Pea Rice, use fresh fava beans with seed coats or fresh peas instead of bok choy.

Congee has a special flavor and smoothness. It is simply delicious.

Pai Chou   白 粥

PLAIN RICE CONGEE

¾ *cup oval-grain rice or* ½ *cup long-grain and* ¼ *cup glutinous rice*
 8 *cups water*

Preparation and Cooking:
Wash and drain the rice several times. To a 2- to 3-quart saucepan, add the washed rice and 8 cups water and bring to a boil. Cook gently over medium heat, partially covered, for 30 minutes. Reduce heat to low. Cover the saucepan and simmer for about 1½ hours or until the contents looks like gruel. (The rice grains absorb all the water and become very soft.) Congee is best served hot, accompanied by small portions of salty and highly seasoned dishes, or one may add some sugar, which will give a soothing and comfortable feeling.

Yield: 4 servings.

Note: Congee can be baked in the oven. Use a heavy ovenproof pot with a tightly fitted lid. Bring the rice and water (6 cups instead of 8) to a boil on top of the stove, then bake in a preheated 225° oven for 2 to 3 hours.

Ts'ai Chou

菜粥

VEGETABLE RICE CONGEE

1 *pound bok choy*
¾ *cup oval-grain rice or ½ cup long-grain and ¼ cup glutinous rice*
6 *cups water*
1 *teaspoon salt*
3 *tablespoons peanut or corn oil*

Preparation and Cooking:
Wash and drain bok choy. Cut the stalk and leaves into ½-inch pieces. Set aside.

Follow the directions for Plain Rice Congee (page 148). After the rice boils for 5 minutes, add the bok choy, salt, and oil. Stir well and return to a boil. Turn heat to low, and let cook for about 1 hour or until the bok choy is very soft and the rice resembles gruel.

Yield: 4 servings.

Variations: Any kind of dried soybean milk products (sheets, sticks, pieces) with seed coats removed, or ginkgo nuts, can be cooked with Plain Rice Congee. Season with salt.

Kuo Pa

RICE PATTIES

鍋巴

1½ *cups long-grain rice*
2 *cups cold water*
2 *cups peanut or corn oil*
   Fine salt to taste

Preparation:
Rinse and drain the rice and put it and the cold water in a 10 x 15-inch jelly roll pan. Spread the rice evenly in a single layer. (The grains should touch each other. If you must use a smaller pan, adjust the quantities of rice and water accordingly.) Let stand for 30 minutes.

Cooking:
Cover the pan with aluminum foil and bake in a preheated 350° oven for 30 minutes. Remove the foil, wet the back of a spatula, and press the rice down firmly. Reduce the heat to 300° and continue baking the rice, uncovered, for about 1 hour. The rice will be dry at the side of the pan, but the center will still be damp.

Take the pan out of the oven and cut the rice with a knife approximately into 3 x 3-inch pieces. You should have about 15 patties. Leave them out overnight, making sure the next morning that the Rice Patties have dried out thoroughly. Thoroughly dried rice patties can be kept in tins for a long time and fried when needed.

Heat the oil in a wok until very hot (about 400°) and fry the dried Rice Patties, 2 pieces at a time, for about 5 seconds on each side. Drain. The patties will be crispy and light brown, and will expand to twice their size. Sprinkle on the fine salt while the patties are still hot. Break into desired-size pieces for snacks or appetizers.

Unsalted fried Rice Patties can be kept in tins. Reheat just before serving in a very hot oven (475°) and use in the recipe for Vegetarian Sizzling Rice Soup or combine with any hot dish with sauce.

Yield: 15 4 x 4-inch fried patties.

Liang Mien Huang   兩 面 黃

TWO-SIDES BROWNED NOODLES

In this dish a bed of noodles is fried in oil in a frying pan. The resulting thin, cakelike noodle patty is brown and has a crunchy crust on both sides. It is still soft inside, however. The other ingredients and the sauce are poured on top of the noodles but not mixed in when served. Thus, one can taste the different flavor of each ingredient with just enough sauce absorbed by the noodles.

  6 *large dried mushrooms*
½ *cup dried flat-tip bamboo shoots*
1½ *cups warm water*
  2 *cups shredded bok choy or other cabbage*
½ *pound fresh egg noodles (about 4 cups cooked)*
  2 *quarts boiling water*
  5 *tablespoons peanut or corn oil*
  1 *tablespoon soy sauce*
½ *teaspoon sugar*
  2 *teaspoons cornstarch*
  1 *teaspoon sesame oil*

Preparation:
Wash the mushrooms and bamboo shoots and soak in the warm water for 1 hour. Squeeze the water out of the vegetables, reserving the water for later use. Finely shred the mushrooms and bamboo shoots and set aside on a plate with the shredded bok choy.

Boil the egg noodles in the boiling water for 2 to 3 minutes. Drain and mix in 1 tablespoon of the oil. Spread on a plate to cool.

Cooking:
Heat a large skillet until very hot. Add 1 tablespoon of the oil to coat the pan. Spread the cooked egg noodles in the skillet, smoothing them down. Move the pan, tipping it from side to side, for about 5 minutes, so that the noodles will shift along the bottom surface of the pan. The noodles will start to brown. Swirl for another 2 minutes, then flip the noodle patty over. Add 1 more tablespoon oil and brown. Transfer to a platter and keep warm in the oven.

Heat a wok or pan and add the remaining 2 tablespoons oil. Stir-fry the mushrooms, bamboo shoots, and bok choy together for 2 minutes or until the vegetables wilt. Add the soy sauce and sugar. Stir to mix. Strain the reserved mushroom-bamboo shoot water and slowly pour about ½ cup of it into the wok. In a cup, combine ¼ cup of the soaking water with the cornstarch. Discard the bottom layer (remaining ¼ cup soaking) water. When the liquid in the wok begins to boil slowly, stir in the well-blended cornstarch mixture. When the ingredients are coated with a light glaze, add the sesame oil and mix well. Pour the vegetables and sauce on top of the hot noodle patty and serve hot.

Yield: 2 servings as lunch, 4 servings as a snack or when served with other dishes.

Note: Flipping the noodles over may take a little practice. An easy way to do it is to simply slide the noodle patty onto a plate and invert the skillet over the uncooked side of the patty. Quickly invert both plate and skillet so that the uncooked side is on the bottom of the pan.

Liang Pan Mien

涼拌麵

NOODLE SALAD

1 *pound fresh or dried egg noodles*
3 *to 4 quarts boiling water*
2 *tablespoons sesame or corn oil*
1 *tablespoon soy sauce*

Preparation and Cooking:
Drop the noodles into a large pot of boiling water and stir to separate them. Boil for about 3 to 4 minutes or until the desired tenderness is reached. Rinse under cold water and drain thoroughly. Spread the noodles to let dry for 10 minutes. Add the oil and soy sauce to the noodles and toss well. Cover and chill in the refrigerator for no more than 2 hours.

Yield: 8 1-cup servings.

Note: Suggested topping includes Shredded Egg Sheets (page 114), shredded cucumbers, radishes, lettuce, or blanched fresh bean sprouts.

Following are two different dressings to be served with Noodle Salad. You may use either or both of them in the same meal. Also, different seasoning ingredients may be set on the table, and each person may make his or her own dressing.

VINEGAR AND SOY SAUCE DRESSING

¼ *cup light soy sauce*
¼ *cup cider vinegar*
2 *tablespoons sesame oil*
2 *teaspoons sugar*
¼ *teaspoon monosodium glutamate*

Preparation:
Blend ingredients and serve in a sauceboat.

PEANUT BUTTER AND PEPPER DRESSING

2 *tablespoons peanut butter or sesame paste*
3 *tablespoons warm water*
2 *tablespoons soy sauce*
1 *tablespoon cider vinegar*
2 *tablespoons sesame or corn oil*
2 *teaspoons Hot Pepper Oil (page 139) or 1 teaspoon cayenne*
   pepper
2 *teaspoons sugar*
½ *teaspoon salt*
¼ *teaspoon monosodium glutamate*
2 *cloves garlic, finely chopped*
2 *tablespoons finely chopped scallion*

Preparation:
Combine the peanut butter or sesame paste with the warm water to make a smooth, thin sauce. Combine with remaining ingredients

except the garlic and scallion into a very smooth dressing. Add the finely chopped garlic and scallion before serving. Serve in a sauceboat.

Note: Peanut Butter and Pepper Dressing is also very good on hot noodles.

T'ang Mi Fan   湯米粉

RICE STICKS IN VEGETABLE SOUP

Rice sticks are noodle-shaped wads made of rice flour. They can be stir-fried or cooked in a tasty vegetable soup. The soup can be served by itself as lunch or a light supper.

Cooking:
Bring the Vegetable Soup (page 134) to a boil and add ½ pound of dried rice sticks. Submerge the rice sticks in the soup then bring to a boil. Adjust the seasoning. Divide the noodles and soup among 4 large bowls. Serve hot.

Yield: 4 servings.

Fa Mien   發麵

YEAST DOUGH

3½ *cups all-purpose flour (approximately)*
 ½ *envelope active dry yeast (about 1⅛ teaspoons)*
 ¼ *cup lukewarm water*
  2 *tablespoons sugar*
  1 *cup lukewarm milk or 1 cup lukewarm water combined with
       1 tablespoon oil*
 ½ *teaspoon baking powder*

Preparation:
Place the flour in a large mixing bowl. Sprinkle the yeast into the lukewarm water. Cover with a saucer and let stand for 5 minutes.

Dissolve the sugar in the lukewarm milk. Mix the yeast mixture well and combine it with the sugared milk, then slowly stir into the flour, forming a firm dough. (Add more flour if dough is sticky). Knead until smooth and leave in the bowl. Cover the bowl and let rise in a warm place for about 2 hours or until doubled in bulk.

Turn out the dough onto a lightly floured surface, and spread it out. Sprinkle the baking powder all over the dough, then knead until smooth and not sticky, about 7 to 8 minutes. Sprinkle flour onto the dough from time to time while kneading. Cover the dough with the bowl and let rest for 10 minutes. Knead again for 1 to 2 minutes. Now it is ready to make different kinds of buns.

Note: An electric mixer with a dough hook may be used, but only if the recipe is doubled. When doubling the recipe, let the dough rise for an extra hour.

Hua Chüan   花 捲

STEAMED FLOWER BUNS

1 *recipe Yeast Dough (page 154)*
1 *tablespoon sesame or peanut oil*

Preparation:
Follow the directions for Yeast Dough. After the rising, kneading, and resting, divide the dough in half. Put one half in a covered bowl. Roll out the other half into a rectangle approximately 10 x 14 inches, and about ⅛ inch thick. With a pastry brush spread a thin coat of the oil over the surface of the dough. Roll up the long side of the dough in a jelly roll fashion into a long, sausagelike shape, about 1 inch in diameter. Cut the roll into pieces ¾ inches long. By placing one on top of another, stack pairs of the round pieces, uncut surfaces touching. With the blunt edge of a knife, press down firmly on each pair to make the rounds adhere to each other. Holding the ends of the rounds together with your thumb and forefingers, gently pull the ends slightly away from the center of the roll and then draw the ends under until they meet. Pinch the ends firmly together to secure them. During this process the oiled layers

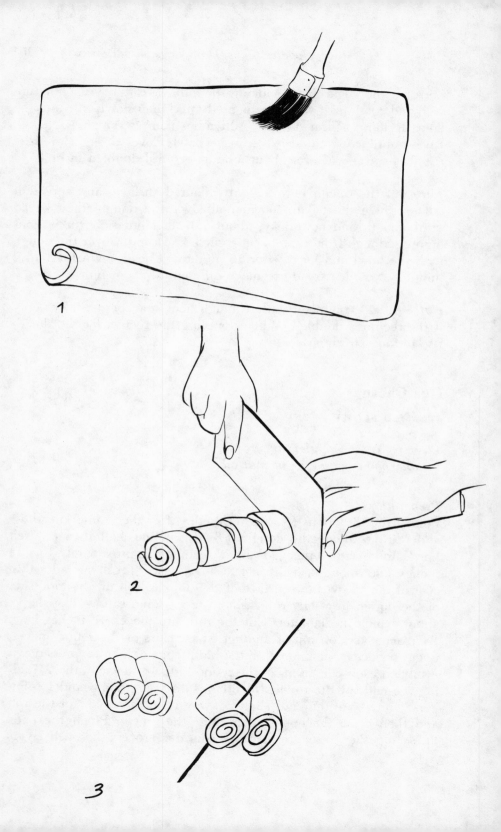

1

2

3

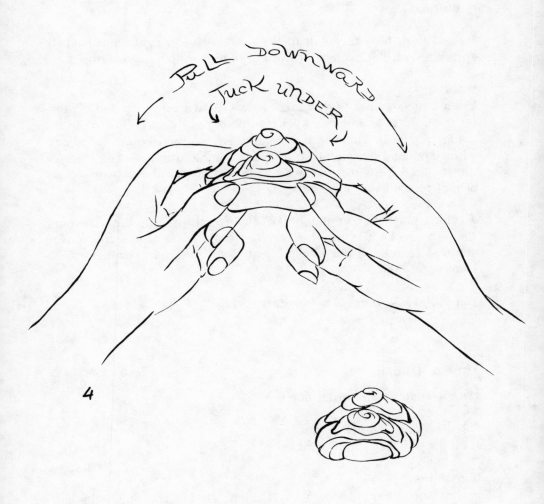

PULL DOWNWARD

TUCK UNDER

4

should separate into rosebud-like "flowers." Place the flower buns on a lightly floured tray. Cover with a dry cloth and let rise for 20 minutes.

Repeat with the other half of the dough. Knead again and slightly sprinkle with flour during kneading before shaping into flowers.

Cooking:
Fill a large steamer with 2 inches water and bring to a boil. Transfer the buns to an oiled rack. Do not pack tightly and allow room for rising. Cover the steamer and steam the buns for 10 minutes. Meanwhile, spread a large cloth towel on the table. Immediately transfer the steamed buns to the towel. This will absorb the extra droplets of moisture on the buns. Serve hot.

To store, let them completely cool before putting into a plastic bag. They can be kept in the refrigerator for a week and in a freezer for months. To reheat, put in a preheated steamer, and steam for 5 to 10 minutes.

Yield: 30 to 35 buns, 2 x 3 inches.

Yin Szu Chüan 銀絲捲

STEAMED SILVER THREAD BUNS

1 *recipe Yeast Dough (page 154)*
1 *tablespoon peanut or corn oil*

Preparation:
Follow the directions for Yeast Dough. Divide the dough in half and keep one half in a covered bowl. Roll out the other half into a 8 x 12-inch rectangle. Cut the long side into 2 6 x 8-inch pieces; cut 1 of the pieces into 2 4 x 6-inch pieces for wrapping. Brush the 6 x 8-inch piece with oil, then lift up the long side and fold once. With a sharp knife cut into fine noodlelike strips from the short end. Use fingers to lift up the 2 ends, 2 strips at a time, and stretch until about 6 inches long, then place on the long sides

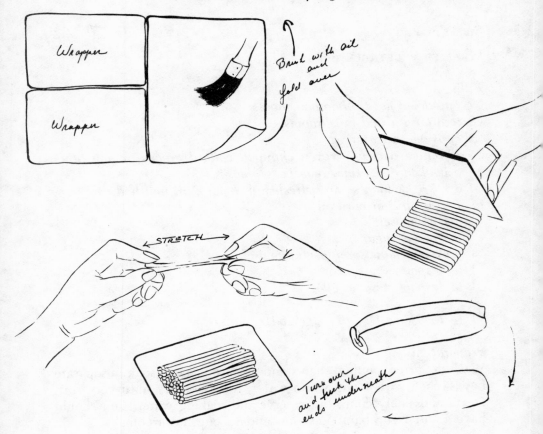

of the 2 wrappers (the 4 x 6-inch pieces) of dough. Roll up the wrappers and noodle strips tightly. Tuck the sides and ends underneath so that they seal when rising. Repeat with the other half of the dough.

Place the finished silver thread buns on a piece of waxed paper. Cover with a dry cloth and let rise for 45 minutes.

Cooking:
Set up a large steamer and bring 2 inches of water to a boil. Transfer the buns to an oiled tier or rack and place in the steamer. Cover and steam over high heat for 20 minutes. Serve hot. For storing directions, see recipe for Steamed Flower Buns (page 155).

Yield: 4 3 x 8-inch buns.

Su Ts'ai Pao

素菜飽

STEAMED VEGETABLE BUNS

Filling:
½ *cup dried flat-tip bamboo shoots*
6 *to 8 large dried mushrooms*
2 *cups warm water*
1 *10-ounce package frozen chopped collard greens or any other*
    cooked or frozen green vegetables
4 *3 x 3 x ¾-inch squares fresh firm bean curd, mashed*
¼ *cup peanut or corn oil*
2 *teaspoons salt*
2 *teaspoons sugar*
¼ *teaspoon monosodium glutamate*
1 *tablespoon soy sauce*
1 *tablespoon sesame oil*

1 *recipe Yeast Dough (page 154)*

Preparation:
Wash the dried bamboo shoots and mushrooms and soak in separate
bowls, each with 1 cup warm water, for 1 hour or until very soft.
Drain and finely chop, but reserve the soaking water. You should
have about 1 cup bamboo shoots and ½ cup mushrooms.

Thaw the collard greens, squeeze out the excess water, and chop
them more finely. Set aside with the bamboo shoots and mushrooms.

Combine the mashed bean curd with the reserved soaking water
in a saucepan, and slowly bring to a boil over medium heat. Continue to boil until almost all the water has evaporated. Set aside.

Heat a wok until very hot. Add the peanut or corn oil, then the
bamboo shoots and mushrooms. Stir-fry for 2 to 3 minutes. Add the
salt, sugar, monosodium glutamate, soy sauce, bean curd, collard
greens, and sesame oil. Cook for 2 more minutes. The entire contents should be moist but should not have excess sauce. Let cool and
use as the filling. You should have about 5 cups.

Set up a large steamer with 2 or 3 tiers. Arrange 2-inch squares of waxed paper, 2 inches apart on the tiers.

Follow the Yeast Dough recipe. Roll the dough into a sausagelike roll. Break or divide into 24 equal-sized pieces and roll into balls, each about 1½ inches in diameter. With the palm of the hand, flatten each into a round, then roll out each round with a small rolling pin into a 3-inch disk. The center of each disk should be thicker than its edge.

Put about 3 tablespoons of filling in the center of each disk. Flute the edges of the disk and gather them together to form a pouch by making pleats with the thumb and forefinger. Set each finished bun on a square of waxed paper. Cover them as they are made and let rise for about 30 minutes.

Cooking:
Fill the steamer with water 2 to 3 inches deep and bring to a boil. Place the two steamer tiers with the vegetable buns over the boiling water and steam over high heat for about 15 minutes.

Yield: 24 3-inch buns.

Variation: For sweet Red Bean Paste Buns, use 1½ tablespoons Red Bean Paste (page 176) for the filling instead of the vegetable filling.

Fu P'i Man T'ou   麩皮饅頭

WHOLE WHEAT BUNS

>   2 *cups whole wheat flour*
>   2 *cups all-purpose flour*
>   1 *envelope dried yeast (about 2¼ teaspoons)*
> 1½ *cups warm water (approximately)*
>   3 *tablespoons sugar*
> ½ *teaspoon salt*
>   2 *tablespoons peanut or corn oil*
>   1 *teaspoon baking powder*

Preparation:
Combine the whole wheat flour and all-purpose flour in a large mixing bowl. Sprinkle the dried yeast into a small bowl with the warm water. Cover with a saucer and let stand for 5 minutes. Add the sugar, salt, and oil to the yeast mixture, mix well, then slowly stir mixture into the flour (add warm water if too dry) to form a soft but not sticky dough. Knead until smooth and return the dough to the bowl. Cover the bowl and let rise in a warm place for about 2 hours or until doubled in bulk.

Set up a large steamer with 2 or 3 steamer tiers. Arrange on each tier 2-inch squares of waxed paper, 2 inches apart.

Turn out the dough onto a lightly floured surface and spread it out. Sprinkle the baking powder all over the dough, then knead for about 7 to 8 minutes. Sprinkle on some flour from time to time during the kneading. Cover the dough with the bowl and let rest for 10 minutes.

Knead the dough for 1 to 2 minutes then roll the dough into a long sausagelike roll about 1 inch in diameter. Cut the roll into 20 1½-inch-long buns. Set the buns on the pieces of waxed paper in the steamer, cover, and let rise for about 40 minutes.

Cooking:
Fill the steamer with water 2 to 3 inches deep, and bring to a boil. Place 2 steamer tiers over the boiling water, cover, and steam the buns over high heat for 20 minutes.

Yield: 20 3-inch buns.

Note: With 1½ or more recipes, the dough may be kneaded with the dough hook of a heavy-duty mixer. Whole Wheat Buns may be split into halves and toasted in the toaster. They may also be frozen and reheated in a steamer.

Yu Su Chiao   油 酥 餃

MUSHROOM PUFFS

Filling:
  3 *tablespoons peanut or corn oil*
  1 *pound fresh mushrooms, thinly sliced (about 6 cups)*
  2 *teaspoons salt*
  ½ *teaspoon sugar*
  1 *tablespoon soy sauce*

Dough:
  2 *cups all-purpose flour*
  ⅔ *cup shortening*
  ⅓ *cup ice water*

  1 *large egg, beaten*

Preparation:
For the filling, heat a wok or pan until hot. Add the oil and the mushrooms. Stir-fry for about 7 to 8 minutes or until the liquid has evaporated. Add the salt, sugar, and soy sauce, and mix and cook some more. The mushrooms should be fairly dry. Remove and let cool, then finely chop the mushrooms. Set aside.

Prepare the dough in a large mixing bowl. Combine the flour with the shortening and work with your fingertips until the shortening is evenly mixed in and the mixture has the texture of cornmeal. Stir in the ice water, mix, and pat into 2 balls.

Cooking:
Roll out the dough, 1 ball at a time, on a lightly floured surface until about 1/16 inch thick. Using a cookie-cutter, cut out circles

about 3 inches in diameter. Knead the scraps together and roll out to make more circles.

Place about 1 teaspoon of filling in the center of each round, fold over to make a half-moon shape, and seal the edges tightly, making scallops with your fingertips. Place the puff on an ungreased baking sheet and prick each puff with a fork. Brush the tops with beaten eggs. Bake in a 400° oven for about 20 minutes or until golden brown.

Yield: Makes about 60 puffs.

Note: The puffs can be frozen before or after baking, and reheated in a 350° oven for 10 minutes.

Shao Mai   燒賣
STEAMED DUMPLINGS

Filling:
 1 *cup glutinous rice*
 2 *cups warm water*
12 *dried mushrooms*
 1 *cup finely chopped bamboo shoots*
½ *cup finely chopped Szechuan preserved vegetable* (Szechuan cha ts'ai)
 4 *tablespoons peanut or corn oil*
 1 *teaspoon salt*
 1 *teaspoon sugar*
¼ *teaspoon monosodium glutamate*

Wrappers:
 2 *cups all-purpose flour*
⅔ *cup 150°-water (hot to the finger but not burning; ⅓ cup boiling water combined with ⅓ cup tap water may be used)*

Preparation:
Wash the rice several times and drain. Put the rice in a heatproof bowl and add 1 cup of the warm water. Let the rice soak in the

water for 30 minutes. Wash the mushrooms and soak in the remaining 1 cup warm water for 30 minutes.

Place the bowl with rice and water on a rack in a pot with several inches of water. The water level should reach about 1½ inches below the bowl's rim. Cover the pot. Bring it to a boil and steam the rice over medium heat for about 30 minutes.

Drain the mushrooms, but reserve ¼ cup of the soaking water. Cut off and discard the mushroom stems, then finely chop the caps. You should have about ⅔ cup. Set aside with the chopped bamboo shoots and Szechuan preserved vegetable.

Heat a wok until very hot. Add the oil, then the bamboo shoots, and stir-fry for 2 to 3 minutes. Add the mushrooms and Szechuan preserved vegetable, and mix with the bamboo shoots. Add the steamed rice, the salt, sugar, monosodium glutamate, and reserved ¼ cup mushroom water. Mix them thoroughly while still cooking over low heat. Remove and set aside, to use as filling.

To prepare the wrappers, place the flour in a large mixing bowl. Add the hot water and stir to mix well to form a pliable but firm dough. Add more hot water if the dough is too dry. Knead the dough until very smooth, then cover with a damp cloth and let stand for about 15 minutes.

Turn out dough onto a lightly floured surface and knead for 5 minutes. Divide it in half. Keep one half covered in a bowl and shape the other half into a sausagelike cylinder about 15 inches long and 1 inch in diameter. Cut into 30 ½-inch pieces. Lay the pieces cut sides down and dust them lightly with flour. Press each piece with the palm of your hand to flatten it. Use a small rolling pin, roll out each piece into a paper-thin disk 2½-inches in diameter. As you roll out the disks, turn clockwise a quarter turn to keep the shape round and the edges thinner than the center. Cover the finished disks with a dry cloth to prevent drying out.

Place about 1 tablespoon of the filling in the center of a disk. Gather the sides of the wrapper around the filling, letting the wrapper form small rippled pleats. Squeeze the middle gently to make sure the

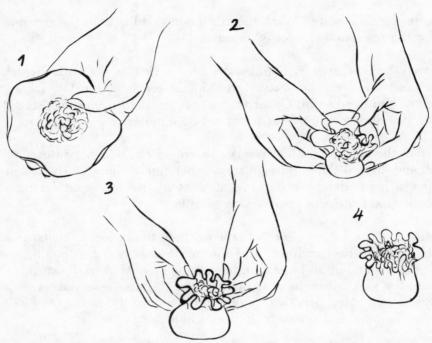

wrapper sticks firmly against the filling, then press down on a flat surface so that the dumpling can stand with the filling exposed at the top. Leave a narrow ruffled border of the wrapper unattached to the filling. Place the dumplings on a greased plate 1 inch smaller in diameter than your steamer.

Finish the other half of the dough in the same fashion.

Cooking:
Fill the steamer with water 2 to 3 inches deep, and bring to a boil. Place the plate with the dumplings on the steamer rack. Cover the pot tightly and steam over medium-high heat for 5 minutes. Serve hot. The dumplings can be reheated by steaming.

Yield: 60 dumplings.

Variation: Sautéed fresh mushrooms may be used instead of dried ones.

Chiao Tzu

餃子

BOILED VEGETABLE DUMPLINGS

Filling:
  5 *tablespoons peanut or corn oil*
  4 *cups finely chopped celery*
  ½ *cup finely chopped bamboo shoots*
  ½ *cup finely chopped soaked dried mushrooms (about 8 large)*
  1 *cup cooked carrots, finely chopped*
  2 *teaspoons salt*
  1 *tablespoon light soy sauce*
  ¼ *teaspoon monosodium glutamate*

Wrappers:
  2 *cups all-purpose flour*
  ⅔ *cup cold water*

Dip:
  2 *tablespoons rice vinegar*
  ¼ *cup soy sauce*

Preparation:
For the filling, heat a wok until very hot. Add the oil, chopped celery and bamboo shoots. Stir-fry for about 5 minutes or until the vegetables are very dry but not brown. Add the mushrooms and carrots, stir, and cook some more. Add the salt, soy sauce, and monosodium glutamate. Mix well. Remove and let cool.

To prepare the wrappers, put the flour in a large mixing bowl and make a well in the center. Gradually add the water, and stir to make a firm dough (it is important to start with a firm dough; if it is too dry, add more water). Knead the dough until it feels smooth and does not stick to your fingers. Place the dough in the bowl and cover with a damp cloth. Let stand for about 15 minutes. The dough can be made ahead of time and kept in a tightly covered container in the refrigerator for up to 2 days.

Turn out the dough onto a lightly floured surface and knead for 5 minutes. Divide it in half. Keep one half covered in a bowl and shape the other half into a sausagelike cylinder, about 10 inches long and 1 inch in diameter. Cut into 15 ⅔-inch-thick pieces. Lay the pieces cut sides down on surface and dust lightly with flour. Press each piece with the palm of your hand to flatten it. Use a small rolling pin to roll each piece into a disk 2½ inches in diameter and about ⅛ inch thick. Turn clockwise a quarter turn as you roll to keep the shape round and the edges thinner than the center. Cover the disks with a dry cloth to prevent drying out.

Place about 1 tablespoon of the filling in the center of each wrapper. Fold over one third of the wrapper, just enough to barely cover the filling. Starting from one end, pinch the edge of the dough, and with the fingers of the other hand, push the extra dough around to the front so that pleats form on the center front, in the shape of a fisherman's creel. Use your thumb and forefinger to press and seal the openings. Arrange the dumplings on a floured tray and cover with a dry cloth and repeat the procedure with the remaining dough.

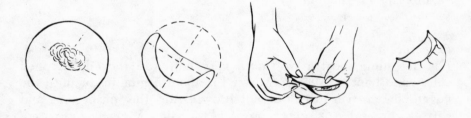

Cooking:
Bring 2 quarts water to a boil in a large pot. Add about 30 vegetable dumplings and stir once. Cover and bring to a boil. Add 1 cup cold water, cover, and wait until the water comes to a boil again. Repeat, adding the cold water in the same manner twice again. When the dumplings float to the top, remove from the boiling water with a strainer. Combine the dip ingredients, and serve with the hot dumplings and Plain Rice Congee (page 148). Or serve the dumpling cooking water as a beverage.

Yield: 30 dumplings, about 4 servings as a lunch or light supper.

Variation: Bok choy, celery cabbage, and other vegetables may be used instead of celery. Sautéed fresh mushrooms may be used instead of dried mushrooms. For another tasty filling, use the filling for Steamed Vegetable Buns (page 160).

Chun Chüan   春捲

SPRING ROLLS (EGG ROLLS)

    8 *large dried mushrooms*
    4 *3 x 3 x ⅓-inch homemade Seasoned Pressed Bean Curd (page
        80) or ready-made*
    4 *cups 2-inch-long pieces of shredded celery*
    1 *cup 2-inch-long pieces of shredded carrots*
 1¼ *cups peanut or corn oil*
    1 *tablesopon light soy sauce*
 1½ *teaspoons salt*
    1 *teaspoon sugar*
   ¼ *teaspoon monosodium glutamate*
    1 *tablespoon sesame oil*
    1 *tablespoon cornstarch*
   20 *ready-made spring roll wrappers, square or round*
    1 *large egg, beaten*

Preparation:
Wash and soak the mushrooms in 1 cup warm water for 30 minutes or until they are soft. Cut off and discard the mushroom stems, then finely shred the caps. Reserve the soaking liquid.

Slice the Seasoned Pressed Bean Curd as thin as possible, then cut again into shreds. You should have about 4 cups. Set aside on a large plate with the celery, carrots, and mushrooms.

Heat a wok until very hot. Add 2 tablespoons of the peanut or corn oil and stir-fry the shredded bean curd and mushrooms for 2 minutes. Add the light soy sauce, mix well, remove, and set aside.

Heat a clean wok and add 2 more tablespoons of the peanut or corn oil. Stir-fry the carrots and celery for 5 minutes or until the vegetables are soft and dry but not brown. Add the salt, sugar, monosodium glutamate, sesame oil, and then the cooked bean curd with the mushrooms, stirring to mix well. Blend the cornstarch with 3 tablespoons of the reserved mushroom soaking water and pour into the contents of the wok. Mix and cook some more. The thickened sauce should coat all the ingredients. Remove and let cool to use as the filling.

Wrapping:
Set aside the beaten egg and a pastry brush. Separate the spring roll wrappers by gently pulling off 1 piece at a time. Keep in a stack, covered with a damp cloth. If the wrappers are too stiff because of long storage, carefully separate them. Wrap a warm cloth around them until they are soft, or steam them over low heat for a few minutes. Then stack and cover with a damp cloth.

Take 1 spring roll wrapper and place on a flat surface. Take about 2 tablespoons of filling and place at the lower corner of the wrapper.

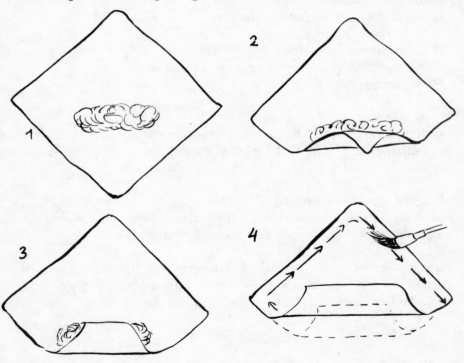

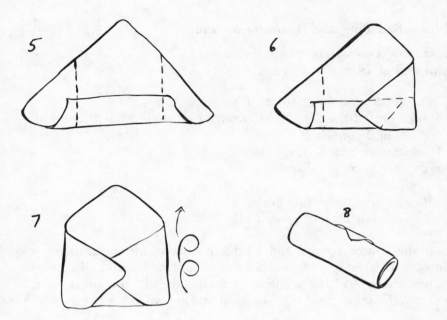

With your hands, shape the filling into a 1-inch long sausage, lift the lower corner over the filling, begin to roll and tuck the edge or point under the filling. Roll into a cylinder about 4 inches long. Brush the exposed edges of the wrapper with the beaten egg. Now roll to the center. Bring the two side corners up over the top of the enclosed filling and gently press down. Continue rolling into a neat 5-inch-long spring roll. The beaten egg will seal the edges and keep the skin intact. Cover with a kitchen towel until ready to cook.

Cooking:
Heat 1 cup peanut or corn oil in a frying pan to about 350°. Place 6 or 7 spring rolls in the oil and fry 5 to 6 minutes or until golden brown and crispy, turning them for even frying. Transfer the Spring Rolls to a paper towel to drain. Keep warm in the oven while the rest of the Spring Rolls are being fried. Serve hot, with vinegar and Hot Pepper Oil (page 139) as dips.

Yield: 20 Spring Rolls.

Note: Spring Rolls can be frozen after frying. They can be reheated (on a rack, not a tray) in a 450° oven for about 10 minutes.

Lo Po Szu Ping and Tou Sha Su Ping 蘿蔔絲餅

SCALLION AND WHITE TURNIP SU PING 豆沙酥餅
AND RED BEAN PASTE SU PING

Filling for Scallion and White Turnips Su Ping:

4 *cups grated Chinese white turnips (not more than 1-inch long),*
   about 2 pounds
1 *tablespoon plus 2 teaspoons salt*
½ *cup finely chopped scallions*
2 *teaspoons sugar*
¼ *teaspoon monosodium glutamate*
2 *tablespoons corn or peanut oil*

Combine grated turnips and 1 tablespoon salt, mix well, then pack down and let stand for 30 minutes. Squeeze out and discard the excess water. Add the scallions, 2 teaspoons salt, the sugar, monosodium glutamate, and oil. Mix well and set aside for use as filling.

Filling for Red Bean Paste Su Ping:

2 *cups homemade Red Bean Paste (page 176) or canned*
1 *large egg, beaten*
½ *cup black or white sesame seeds*
3 *to 4 cups peanut or corn oil*

DOUGHS FOR SU PING:
Dough with Shortening:
1 *cup all-purpose flour*
⅓ *cup shortening (approximately)*

Mix flour with shortening into a soft, light dough (add more shortening if dough is dry).

Dough with Water:
2⅓ *cups flour*
½ *cup shortening (at room temperature)*
⅔ *cup cold water (approximately)*

Place flour on work surface. Make a well in the center and add the shortening, and about ¼ cup cold water to the well. Start incorporating the 3 ingredients and gradually add more water. Keep working the dough until all the dry flour is mixed in. Add just enough water until a soft but not sticky dough is formed. Knead the dough until smooth.

Roll the two kinds of dough separately into two 12-inch-long rolls and cut each roll into 12 pieces. Roll out each piece of Dough with Water into a 3-inch round. Put one piece of Dough with Shortening in each round and wrap to seal, so that the dough completely surrounds the shortening dough. Repeat with the other 11 pieces.

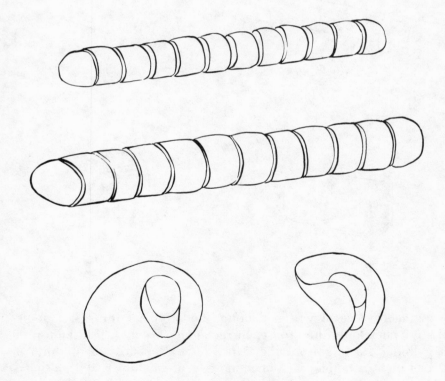

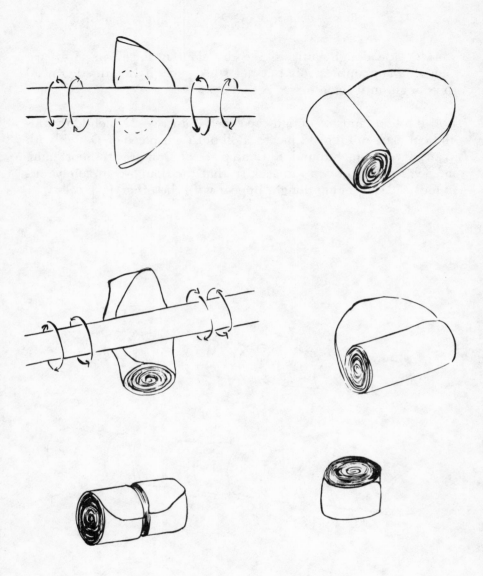

Take each piece of wrapped dough and roll out into a rectangle
2 x 6-inches long, then roll each rectangle in jelly roll fashion into
a cylinder starting from the 2-inch side. Repeat; roll out into a
2 x 14-inch rectangle, then once more form a cylinder. With a sharp
knife cut each cylinder in half lengthwise or crosswise. Put the cut

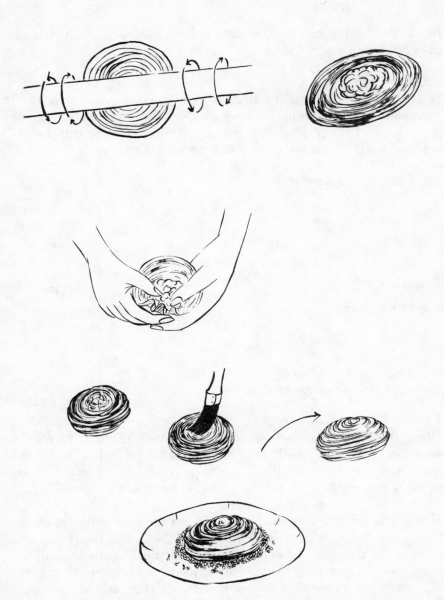

side down and roll out with the rolling pin into rounds 3 inches in
diameter. Place 1 tablespoon of either filling in the center. Gather
up the edge of the round dough to enclose the filling. The finished
ping can be round or oval in shape. Set aside, covered, while you
finish the rest of the *ping* (total 24 *su ping*).

Brush the beaten egg on the gathered side of each finished *ping*, then coat with sesame seeds.

Cooking:
Heat the oil to about 250°. Fry the *ping*, seeded side down, until pale gold, about 10 minutes (the oil should completely cover the *ping* during frying). Drain on paper towels. The *ping* may be reheated in 300° oven for 15 minutes. Serve hot or warm.

Yield: 24 2½-inch *su ping*.

Tou Sha   豆 沙

RED BEAN PASTE

   1 *pound dried red beans*
   2 *quarts water*
1¼ *cups sugar*
1¼ *cups peanut or corn oil*

Preparation and Cooking:
Check over the beans and discard the bad ones. Wash and soak the beans in a large pot with the water for about 4 hours. Bring the water to a boil and cook the beans over low heat for about 2 hours or until the beans are very soft and the water has evaporated.

Use a food processor or food mill to grind the cooked beans into a paste. Put the bean paste and the sugar in a 3- to 4-quart pot. Put an asbestos pad on a burner. Cook over medium-low heat until the bean paste begins to get dryer. Stir once in a while to avoid burning the beans, about 30 minutes to 1 hour. Then add the oil little by little and continue cooking until the paste does not stick to one's finger when touched. Let cool. The paste is now ready to be used as a filling. Leftover bean paste can be stored in the refrigerator or frozen.

Yield: 6 cups.

Tou Sha Tsung

豆沙粽

BAMBOO LEAVES STUFFED WITH RED BEAN PASTE

  3 *cups glutinous rice (sweet rice)*
24 *pieces dried bamboo leaves* (tsung je)
12 *3-foot long pieces thin cotton string*
1½ *cups homemade Red Bean Paste (page 176) or canned*
     Sugar to taste (optional)

Preparation:
Wash the rice several times. Drain and allow it to dry completely.

Rinse the bamboo leaves under running water. Soak in hot water in a baking pan for about 30 minutes. Using scissors, cut off 1 inch at the leaf base. (The softened leaves can be soaked under cold water and drained to be used anytime.)

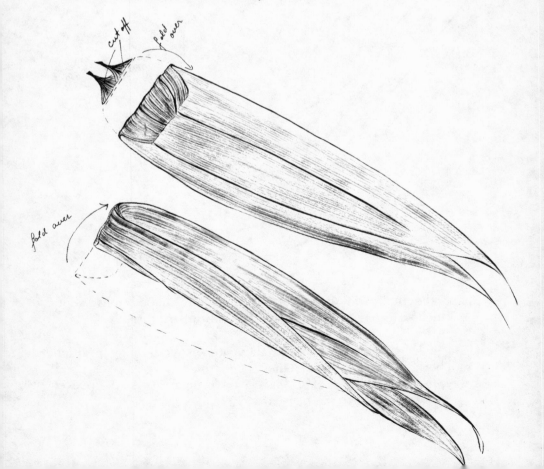

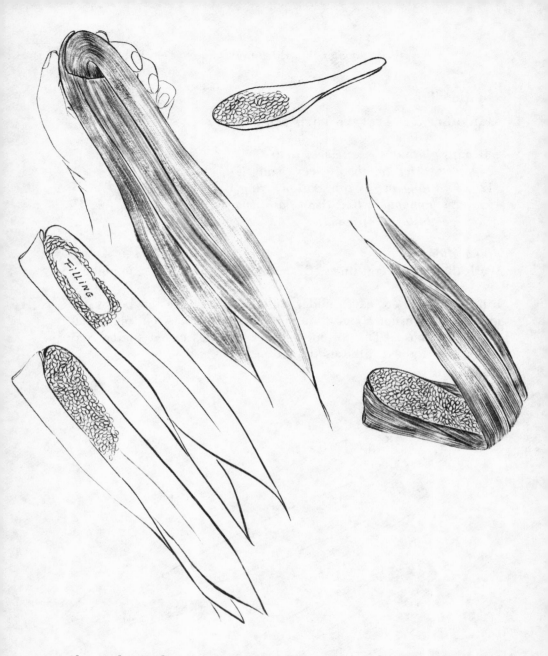

Shape the Red Bean Paste into 12 croquette-shaped rolls, about 1 x 3 inches, to use as filling. Have the cotton string ready.

Using 2 leaves at a time, place them in an overlapping position. Fold both leaves lengthwise then bend the base of leaves about 1 inch to make a long pocket. Place 1 tablespoon rice in the pocket,

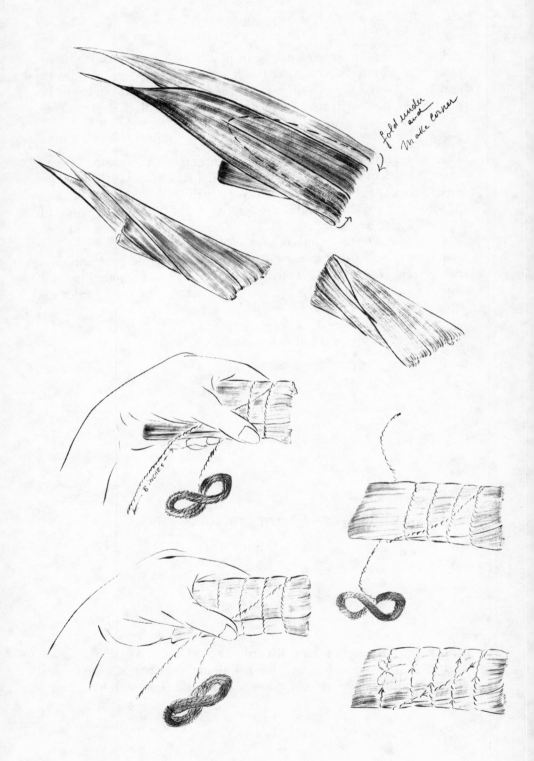

fold under
and
make corner

6 INCHES

filling a 3-inch space. Place 1 bean paste roll on the rice, then add more rice to cover. Now fold the leaves over to cover. Secure the end by folding over. Use the string to tie into a neat package. Repeat procedure with remaining leaves, rice, and Red Bean Paste.

Cooking:
Place the stuffed bamboo leaves in a large pot. Add water to cover the stuffed leaves by 1 inch. Cover and bring to a boil. Cook over medium heat for 1 hour, then turn heat down to low and cook for 3 hours. The water should always cover the bamboo leaves (add boiling water when necessary). They are now ready to eat; untie the string and open the top parts of the leaves and eat the rice and bean paste only. Add sugar to taste if desired. The stuffed bamboo leaves can be reheated either in a steamer for 20 minutes or boiled in water for 10 minutes. They keep well up to 2 weeks in the refrigerator and up to 3 months in the freezer if well wrapped.

Yield: 12 servings as a lunch or snack.

Hong Tou Tsung

紅 豆 粽

BAMBOO LEAVES STUFFED WITH RED BEANS

⅔ *cup dried red beans*
 2 *cups glutinous rice (sweet rice)*
24 *pieces dried bamboo leaves* (tsung je)
12 *3-foot long pieces thin cotton string*

Preparing and Cooking:
Check over the beans and discard the bad ones. Wash the beans and soak in cold water for about 4 hours. Wash the rice several times. Drain both items and allow them to dry completely.

Combine the beans and rice. Follow the directions for Bamboo Leaves Stuffed with Red Bean Paste (page 176) for preparing the bamboo leaves, wrapping, and cooking. Since Bamboo Leaves Stuffed with Red Beans consists of plain beans with rice, they may be served hot and eaten dipped in granulated sugar or sliced when cold, coated with beaten egg, and then pan fried and served with sugar.

Yield: 12 servings as a lunch or snack.

Tsao Ni Hun Tun   棗泥餛飩

DATE WON TONS

Filling:
   1 8-ounce package pitted dates
 ½ cup finely chopped walnuts
   2 teaspoons grated orange rind

   1 pound Cantonese egg roll wrappers, each cut into 9 squares
   2 cups peanut or corn oil
   2 tablespoons confectioners' sugar

Preparation and Cooking:
Cut the dates into fine pieces and combine with the walnuts and orange rind. Wet your hands with some water and shape the filling into small cylinders, about 1 inch long and ⅓ inch in diameter.

Place 1 roll of filling at one corner of a square of egg roll wrapper and roll up. Use water to seal, then twist both free ends to enclose the filling. Heat the oil until hot and deep-fry the won tons over medium-high heat until golden and crispy, about 4 to 5 minutes. Drain on paper towels. Use a small sieve to sprinkle on the confectioners' sugar before serving. See illustration on page 182.

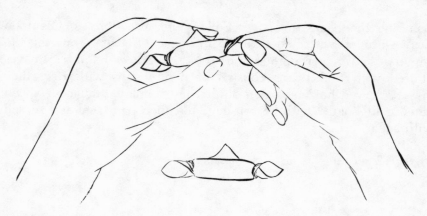

Yield: 150 won tons.

Note: Cover the egg roll wrappers with a damp towel during the wrapping. The fried date won tons can be kept in a covered container for up to 2 weeks. Sprinkle on the confectioners' sugar before serving.

Variation: Cooked jujubes (Chinese red dates) may be used instead of regular dates.

Tou Sha P'in Kuo   豆沙蘋菓

BAKED APPLES WITH RED BEAN PASTE

6 *red delicious apples, about 2½ inches in diameter*
1 *cup homemade Red Bean Paste (page 176) or canned*

Preparation and Cooking:
Preheat the oven to 350°. Cut a ¼-inch thick slice off the top of each apple and save them to use as lids. Remove the core and some pulp of each apple until you have a ⅓-inch-thick shell. Fill the shell about half full with the Red Bean Paste. Replace the apple tops.

Place the filled apples in a baking dish with ¾ cup water. Bake for 30 minutes or until tender. Serve hot.

Yield: 6 servings as a dessert

K'uie Hua T'ang Ou

桂花糖藕

STUFFED LOTUS ROOTS

½ *cup glutinous rice (sweet rice)*
 2 *large center sections fresh lotus roots (with knots intact on both
      sides)*
¼ *cups crushed rock sugar*
 1 *teaspoon sweet olive blossom syrup* (k'uie hua) *(optional)*

Preparation:
Wash the glutinous rice in cold water several times. Drain and dry
thoroughly. Set aside.

Wash the lotus roots, drain, and dry well. Cut off one root end of
each lotus root not more than ½ inch and save it to use as a lid.
Stuff the dried glutinous rice into the lotus root cavities. Make sure
each cavity is tightly filled with rice. Use a chopstick to push down
the rice. Use 3 to 4 toothpicks to secure the reserved end to the
body section.

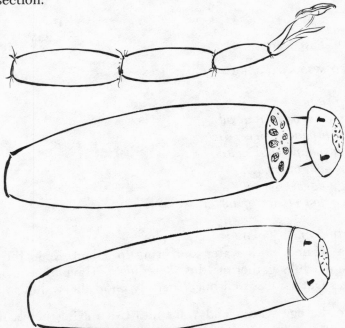

Cooking:

Put the stuffed lotus roots in a pot just large enough that both ends can touch the sides of the pot. Add a bowl of water to weigh down the roots, so that the rice will not fall out while cooking. Add water to cover by about 2 inches above the roots and cook over low heat for about 4 hours, or until the lotus roots are very tender. Use an asbestos pad on the burner. In the last 30 minutes the liquid should be absorbed by the rice.

Take out the lotus roots and peel off the dark skins. Let the cooked lotus roots cool completely, then cut into ¼-inch slices and arrange in a deep dish. Sprinkle the crushed rock sugar and sweet olive syrup on top and cover with plastic wrap. Bring 2 inches water to a boil on a steamer, place the lotus roots on a tier, and steam for at least 30 minutes. Serve hot.

Yield: 8 servings as a dessert.

Note: The dish can be reheated in the steamer and served hot.

Ho T'ao Tan Kao   核桃蛋糕

STEAMED WALNUT CAKE

    ¾ *cup sugar*
    ¼ *cup corn or peanut oil*
   1¼ *cup Japanese sweet rice flour*
    6 *tablespoons cold water*
    ½ *cup walnut meats*
    3 *large eggs*
    ⅛ *teaspoon cream of tartar*

Preparation and Cooking:

Set up a steamer with water and bring to a boil. Keep the water simmering while gathering the ingredients. Have the sugar, oil, flour, and water measured out. Coarsely chop the walnuts.

Separate the egg whites and yolks into two mixing bowls. In one bowl beat the egg whites with the cream of tartar until stiff but not dry. In the other bowl, beat the egg yolk until light yellow in color, then gradually add the sugar and oil while beating. Alternating, add the rice flour and water. Mix and beat some more. Fold in the egg whites. Add the walnuts and blend into the batter. Pour the mixture into a 6- to 8-inch square or round aluminum foil cake pan and steam over high heat for 1 hour, adding more boiling water to the steamer as needed.

Let the cake cool somewhat, cut into thin slices, and serve warm or at room temperature. The cake can be reheated in the steamer after slicing, and served hot.

Yield: 8 servings as a dessert.

Variation: Finely grind the walnut and add ½ cup coarsely cut-up soaked, pitted jujubes (red dates).

Tsao Tzu Nien Kao   棗子年糕

STEAMED GLUTINOUS RICE FLOUR WITH JUJUBES CAKE

This is a typical Chinese cake, particularly in its texture, which is slightly chewy but not sticky. The cake is usually served during the New Year holiday season. No egg is used in this cake, which is flavored with dates.

      1 *cup light brown sugar*
1⅓ *cups warm water*
      4 *ounces cooked pitted jujubes (red dates)*
      1 *pound Chinese glutinous rice flour or Japanese sweet rice flour*
 ⅓ *cup corn oil*

Preparation:
Dissolve the brown sugar in the warm water. Coarsely cut the jujubes and set aside.

Pour the rice flour into a large mixing bowl. Add the oil slowly, then add the sugar-water while beating. The consistency should be like that of mashed potatoes. Fold in the dates, then pour into an 8-inch round cake pan lined with plastic wrap.

Cooking:
Set up a steamer with plenty of boiling water. Steam the cake for 1 hour over medium-high heat. Add more boiling water to the steamer when needed. Serve warm when freshly made or let cool and serve at room temperature.

Yield: 10 to 12 servings as a dessert.

Note: The cake can be kept in the refrigerator for several weeks and in the freezer for several months. It can be reheated in a steamer or toaster oven, or lightly browned with or without oil in a frying pan. Serve hot.

Hsing Jen Ping   杏仁餅

ALMOND COOKIES

    ½ *pound shortening*
    ¾ *cup sugar*
    2 *large eggs*
    2 *teaspoons almond extract*
    4 *drops yellow food coloring*
2½ *cups flour*
    ½ *teaspoon baking soda*
    ¼ *teaspoon salt*
    1 *beaten large egg*
    ½ *cup blanched almonds, split in half*

Preparation:
Cream the shortening and sugar in a large mixing bowl. Beat in 2 eggs, 1 at a time, then add the almond extract and food coloring. In another bowl combine the flour, baking soda, and salt, and mix well. Gradually add to the large bowl, mix, and use your hands to form a fairly firm dough. Divide the dough in half and shape it into two fat cylinders, then roll them on a lightly floured surface into cylinders 14 inches long and 1½ inches in diameter. Wrap them in wax paper and freeze for 30 minutes.

Cooking:
Preheat the oven to 375°. Cut the chilled dough crosswise into slices ¼ inch thick, and arrange on a cookie sheet. Brush with the beaten egg and press an almond half gently in the center of each cookie. Bake in the oven for 10 minutes or until they are golden brown.

Yield: 8 dozen cookies.

Chih Ma Ping Kan   芝蔴餅乾

SESAME SEED COOKIES

½ *cup white sesame seeds*
½ *cup shortening*
¾ *cup sugar*
1 *large egg*
2 *cups flour*
1 *teaspoon baking powder*
¼ *teaspoon salt*
2 *tablespoons cold water*

Preparation:
Toast the sesame seeds in a dry frying pan until they brown lightly and smell fragrant.

In a large mixing bowl cream the shortening until light, gradually adding the sugar while beating. Add the egg and beat until well blended. Add ⅓ of the toasted sesame seeds and mix well. In another bowl combine the flour with the baking powder and salt, and add to the shortening mixture alternately with the cold water. Mix well.

Divide the dough in half and shape into two fat cylinders. Roll these on a lightly floured surface into two neat, smooth cylinders, each about 9 inches long and 1½ inch in diameter. Wrap with waxed paper and freeze for 30 minutes.

Cooking:
Preheat the oven to 350°. Grease 2 cookie sheets. Turn the cookie dough out onto a cutting board and peel off the paper. Cut the dough into slices about ⅛ inch thick. Arrange the cookies on the cookie sheets and sprinkle with the remaining toasted sesame seeds, pressing the seeds into the dough. Bake in the oven for 15 minutes or until lightly browned.

Yield: 6 dozen cookies.

Hsing Jen Lou

杏仁露

ALMOND CREAM

    ¾ *cup large blanched almonds*
  1½ *tablespoons long- or short-grain rice*
    4 *cups cold water*
    6 *tablespoons sugar or to taste*
    1 *tablespoon almond extract*
    1 *12 x 14-inch muslin bag*

Preparation:
Rinse the almonds and rice together. Soak in 2 cups of the cold water for at least 4 hours. Pour almonds and rice with the water into a blender. Blend for 5 minutes or until the liquid is no longer grainy.

With a pot underneath, pour the liquid into the muslin bag. Close the top of the bag by twisting it, then squeeze the bag to extract the almond cream into the pot. Put 1 cup of the cold water in another pot and squeeze the bag again to extract more cream. With the remaining cup of water, repeat the process once more. You should have a total of 4 cups of almond cream. Pour into a saucepan. Discard the residue in the bag and wash the bag for future use.

Cooking:
Heat the saucepan of almond cream. Add the sugar and almond extract, and *slowly* bring to a boil over medium-low heat, stirring constantly. This takes about 15 minutes. It is important that the cream be heated slowly or else it will curdle. Remove from the heat. Serve hot.

Yield: 6 to 8 servings as a dessert or snack.

Note: This can be made ahead of time, reheated, and served hot. It also can be served cold, if you prefer.

Chih Ma Kuo Cha

芝蔴鍋炸

FRIED CUSTARD

¼   *cup white sesame seeds*
½   *cup sugar*

Custard Batter:
½   *cup flour*
 2   *tablespoons cornstarch*
⅔   *cup cold water*
 1   *large egg, beaten*

1½   *cups water*
½   *cup cornstarch*
 2   *cups peanut or corn oil*

Preparation:
Toast the sesame seeds in a frying pan until golden brown. Let cool, then finely crush with a rolling pin on a piece of waxed paper. Mix the crushed sesame seeds with the sugar. Set aside to use to sprinkle over the fried custard.

In a large mixing bowl, combine the flour, cornstarch, and the ⅔ cup cold water, and mix well until smooth. Add the beaten egg and mix some more. There should not be any lumps.

Heat a wok, add the 1½ cups water, and bring to a boil. Slowly pour the batter into the boiling water, using a wire whisk to stir in one direction. Stir until the mixture has an elastic consistency. Pour the entire contents into a greased 5- to 6-inch square cake pan. The custard will fill the pan to a depth of about ¾ inch. Let cool, then place in the refrigerator until firmly set.

Cooking:
Cut the custard into 2 x ¾ x ¾ -inch sticks. You should have about 24 sticks. Lightly roll the sticks in the cornstarch. Heat a wok, add oil and heat to about 375°. Deep fry the coated custard for 3 to 4 minutes or until a light brown crust forms and they are very crisp. Drain and set on a dish. Sprinkle the sesame seed–sugar mixture over the custard and serve hot.

Yield: 6 servings as a dessert.

The Chinese like hot desserts after their banquet meals, or as snacks in soup form. Following are some examples.

Kuei Yuan T'ang   桂圓湯

LONGAN WITH TAPIOCA

 2 *ounces dried seedless longan (dragon's eyes)*
 2 *tablespoons pearl tapioca*
 ¼ *cup sugar*

Preparation:
Soak the dried longan in water to cover for at least 2 hours. Drain the longan, but reserve and measure the soaking water; add more water, to make 3 cups.

Cooking:
Combine the diluted soaking water and drained longan. In a saucepan, bring to a boil, reduce heat, simmer for 5 minutes. Add the tapioca and stir well. Simmer together for 15 minutes more. Add the sugar and mix well. Serve hot.

Yield: 6 servings as a dessert.

Variations: Longan may be cooked plain or combined with cooked silver ears (use about ½ cup dried silver ears and cook in water for about 3 hours or until soft, then combine).

Hung Tsao Lo Tou T'ang   紅棗綠豆湯

JUJUBES WITH MUNG BEANS SWEET SOUP

½ cup barley
1 cup jujubes (red dates)
1 cup mung beans
3½ quarts water
¾ cup sugar or to taste

Preparation and Cooking:
Wash the barley and jujubes and soak in separate bowls for 1 hour. Check over the mung beans and discard the bad ones. Wash and drain.

Drain the barley and jujubes and rinse in cold water several times. Combine the barley with the mung beans in a large pot. Add 3 quarts of the water and cook over medium heat for 30 minutes, then lower the heat, cover, and cook for 2 to 3 hours.

Place the jujubes in a small saucepan with the remaining 2 cups water and cook over low heat for about 1 hour. When the mung beans and barley are done, add the cooked jujubes, including their cooking liquid, and cook together for 5 minutes. Add sugar to taste. Serve hot or cold. This soup can be served very cold during hot weather as a snack, for breakfast, or for dessert.

Yield: 10 cups or servings.

Note: Do not swallow the thick skins and pits of the jujubes, but use the tongue and teeth to discard them.

Chü Keng

橘羹

SWEET ORANGE SOUP

  ½ *cup fish-eye tapioca, each about* ¼ *inch in diameter*
2½ *cups water*
  1 *naval orange*
  ¼ *cup sugar*

Preparation:
In a bowl soak the tapioca in ½ cup of the water for at least 4 hours or until the water is absorbed.

Using a paring knife, peel the orange to remove the skin and white membrane from each section (reserve the juice). Cut the pulp into small pieces. Put the pulp and juice in a bowl.

Cooking:
In a saucepan combine the sugar and the remaining 2 cups water. Bring to a boil and stir until the sugar is dissolved. Pour in the soaked tapioca, stir, and cook over moderate heat for about 2 minutes or until the tapioca is transparent and soft. Add the cut-up orange and its juice, and mix well. Serve hot.

Yield: 4 servings as a dessert or snack.

Variations: Pearl tapioca may be used instead of fish-eye tapioca (soak only 30 minutes). As a substitute for tapioca, use ½ cup glutinous rice flour or Japanese sweet rice flour, mixed with about ⅕ cup water, to form a soft dough. Break into small pieces and roll between the palms of your hands to make large pea-size balls. Add to the hot sugar water, let boil for 1 minute or until they float on top, then add the cut-up orange and its juice.

A Glossary of Chinese Ingredients

VEGETABLES

Fresh Vegetables

For use in their diet, the Chinese have developed a great variety of vegetables through centuries of experimentation. Some are cultivated, but others are indigenous vegetation that is foraged throughout the countryside. Tender leaf buds of certain trees and bushes are considered prize delicacies, while others are merely seasonal vegetables. The Chinese have learned to use most edible indigenous vegetation, going as far as to reach under water to find edible leaves and roots which are both nutritious and delicious. The list below deals with only a fraction of the vegetables used in Chinese cooking. Although most of them are available year round, each vegetable is generally most flavorful at certain stages of its growth. Some of these vegetables are available in supermarkets; others are sold only in Chinese markets.

Leafy greens can be stored in the refrigerator double-wrapped—first in a brown paper bag, then sealed in a plastic one—for as long as three weeks if the vegetable is bought fresh and stored without excess moisture.

Chinese Cabbage

白菜
Pai Ts'ai

Pai ts'ai and bok choy in Chinese are the same written words. They are names loosely used for different vegetables with pale yellow to dark green leaves on white stems.

Bok Choy

青菜
Ch'ing Ts'ai

Ch'ing ts'ai in Shanghai or bok choy in Cantonese means a fully grown member of this cabbage family. *Ch'ing ts'ai* is marketed at a stage of growth in which it is a most economical purchase. Its taste is bland, but it is the best buy of this group of vegetables. Most of the Chinese restaurants use it as one of their vegetables.

Ch'ing ts'ai is the most important leafy vegetable in Chinese cooking. There are many species of this plant that look like swiss chard; some grow only in the early spring and others are able to survive cold weather. Around New York City, if the winter is not severe, a flavorful rape from *ch'ing ts'ai* that was left on the ground from the previous year will come up in the early spring. Some varieties of *ch'ing ts'ai* have white stems and others have light green stems. The shape of the leaves also varies; some are curly and others are flat or smooth. The leaves in the center of the *ch'ing ts'ai* may grow loosely wrapped and others may grow straight up or spread flat on the ground. *Ch'ing ts'ai* is eaten during all stages of growth, from seedlings to the tender stems from which buds and blossoms begin to grow, and is harvested before it begins to seed. Different names are given to different species and different stages of growth.

Ch'ing Ts'ai Seedlings

雞毛菜

Chi Mao Ts'ai

The Chinese call *ch'ing ts'ai* seedlings "chicken feather vegetable" simply because this name describes their shape. *Ch'ing ts'ai* seedlings have a refreshing flavor, and are used for fillings after being finely chopped or as greens for soups. It is sold by the bunch or by weight in the spring.

Vegetable Heart

菜心

Ts'ai Hsin

Vegetable heart is the equivalent of the heart of celery in *ch'ing ts'ai*—the center of the vegetable. It is the tenderest, juiciest, and best tasting part of the entire *ch'ing ts'ai* and, of course, the most expensive. On special occasions such as banquets, restaurants may be willing to prepare a dish of *ts'ai hsin*, a very special treat.

Oil Vegetable

油菜

Yu Ts'ai

Oil vegetable is a species of *ch'ing ts'ai* that is grown for the oil in its seeds. Hence it is called *yu ts'ai*. It is a very tasty vegetable. It has green stems and long, oval-shaped leaves with small, four-petal yellow blossoms. It has a comparatively stronger but refreshing flavor. Its quality is better than that of *ch'ing ts'ai* and its cost is comparable to that of *ts'ai hsin*.

Mustard Greens

芥菜

Chieh Ts'ai

Chieh ts'ai also belongs to the cabbage family, and there are many varieties. The leaves and stems of one kind may be long and slender; another may be loosely wrapped into a head. A third may have thick, wide stems and wide ruffled leaves. Whatever their shape, Chinese mustard greens all have about the same taste, which is stronger than *ch'ing ts'ai* but with a touch of bitterness. All of them have dark chartreuse stems and leaves. *Chieh ts'ai* is available year round and easily found in Chinese markets.

Chinese Celery Cabbage

天津白菜
山東白菜

Tientsin or
Shantung
Pai Ts'ai

Chinese celery cabbage is another very important vegetable in Chinese cooking. It is at its peak season in late fall and winter. Many varieties of this celery look like cabbage. It has white stems and green outer leaves, but they are usually removed before it reaches the grocery shelves. Two-thirds of Chinese celery cabbage consists of stems and the remainder is leaves. The leaves are pale yellow and the stems are white. The curly leaves are tightly wrapped into an elongated head. The length of this vegetable depends on the variety, but it may be between eight to sixteen inches. In the United States Chinese celery cabbage is commonly known as Chinese celery or celery cabbage, and has become almost as popular as mung bean sprouts. Chinese celery cabbage can be bought in many supermarkets. In China, depending on the region and variety, it is called by several names. For instance, in the North it is called *Tientsin* or *Shangtung pai ts'ai,* in Chekiang and Kiangsu it is called *Huang ya ts'ai,* and in the South around Canton, it is called *Shao ts'ai.* Chinese celery cabbage has a delightful delicate flavor, and can be used in soups and salads, or cooked and served by itself. If it is properly wrapped, this vegetable can be stored for several weeks in the refrigerator.

黃芽菜

Huang Ya Ts'ai

紹菜

Shao Ts'ai

Red-in-Snow

Refer to page 204.

Celery

芹菜

Ch'in Ts'ai

The species of celery used in Chinese cooking has a stronger flavor than pascal celery. It has slender stems with tough fibers. One must be careful in preparing this vegetable to remove the tough parts and cut it into short sections. It is an expensive vegetable but its good flavor makes it worthwhile. *Ch'in ts'ai* can be found most of the time in Chinese markets.

Sweet Fennel

茴香菜

Hui Hsiang Ts'ai

Although the Italian and Chinese cuisines are quite different, many of their vegetables, such as fava beans and green gourd *(hu lu)* are interchangeable. The Chinese often use fennel seeds as a spice but other varieties of fennel, such as the Florence fennel and sweet fennel, are not used as vegetables in Chinese cooking. However, fennel is quiet suitable for cooking in a Chinese-style dish. The part used is the enlarged base which looks almost like a bulb. It has the taste of both anise and celery. When eaten raw, it tastes sweet and its texture is crispy. It is often found in supermarkets.

Amaranth

莧菜
Hsien Ts'ai

Amaranth comes with either a green or red stem, and dark green leaves. Like spinach, its seedlings can be eaten. But as the plant grows, the tender stems and leaves are chopped off for consumption in late spring and through the summer. It is sold by the bunch in Chinese markets.

Chrysanthemum
Greens

茼蒿菜
Tung Hao Ts'ai

Edible chrysanthemums are also called crown daisy. Although cultivated, it grows like a weed. It should be eaten before it begins to bloom. The seedlings are eaten at first, and as it grows this vegetable is harvested by picking off the top several inches of the stem where the leaves and stems are still tender. It is sold by the bunch or by weight. It can be homegrown in almost any type of soil.

Lycium Chinense

枸杞頭
Kou Chi T'ou

枸杞子
Kou Chi Tsu

Kou chi is a shrub, commonly grown in the United States for hedges. It can be found growing wild along the parkways. *Kou chi t'ou* consists of the young shoots and leaves picked off the branches in the early spring. It is used as a green vegetable. It has a special flavor, and is available in Chinese markets when in season. *Kou chi tsu* is the dried red seeds of the *Lycium chinense*. In folk medicine, it is given to people with eye disease.

Chinese Leeks

韭菜
Chiu Ts'ai

The Chinese leek is a perennial plant allied to the onion. Its dark green grasslike leaves are used for flavoring and sometimes as a vegetable. Only fresh Chinese leeks are available, and are sold by the bunch in Chinese vegetable stores. They have a strong aroma and spoil easily. They should be stored in the refrigerator in a double bag (place first in a paper bag, then in a plastic one). Depending upon the freshness of the leeks, they can be kept up to a week.

Soybean Sprouts

Refer to "Soybeans and Other Legumes Products" (page 208).

Mung Bean
Sprouts

Refer to "Soybeans and Other Legumes Products" (page 208).

Sprouted
Fava Beans

Refer to "Soybeans and Other Legumes Products" (page 208).

Chinese
White Turnip

白蘿蔔
Pai Lo Bo

Many varieties of white turnips are suitable for Chinese cooking. The best flavor comes from the large ones, which the Japanese call "daikon." They are about eight inches long and two to three inches in diameter. This type of turnip can be cooked tender without becoming mealy. The best turnips are found in the fall before the heavy frost; at this time they are sweet and juicy. Freezing weather makes the turnip become hollow, and although it is edible its texture is not as good. Sometimes a network of fiber will be found under the peel of the *lo bo* if it was left in the ground too long. It still makes for good eating, however, just peel off the tough fibers and cook in the usual manner.

Light Green Gourd

葫蘆
Hu Lu

This gourd is called by many names describing its shape. Depending on growing conditions, it may be straight or crooked; sometimes it can be as big and as heavy as a baseball bat. Shanghai people call it the night-blooming blossom, because its flowers begin to bloom at dusk. This gourd may be eaten when it is very young, and still fuzzy, and until they are very big. In order to bring out its delicate flavor, the gourd has to be cooked until tender. It may be found in Chinese and Italian markets in the summer.

Hair Melon

結瓜
Chieh Kua

This dark green fuzzy squash is about ten to twelve inches long and three or four inches in diameter. It has a similar texture as the *hu lu,* but a slightly different, blander taste. It is cooked in the same manner as the green gourd, and is available year round in Chinese markets only.

Bitter Melon

苦瓜
K'u Kua

This bitter squash, which has lumps similar to those of the ornamental gourds, are about six to eight inches long and one and a half inches in diameter. When this melon is young, it is light green; as it matures, it becomes darker. The degree of green color depends on its maturity. The older it is the more bitter it will be. People in the south of China enjoy it very much. When it is out of season, it can be very expensive. It is available only in Chinese markets.

Luffa

絲瓜
Szu Kua

Luffa is a dark green squash with either vertical grooves or prominant ribs. It is between ten to fourteen inches long and enlarged at the blossom end. Sometimes it is also called the vegetable sponge. When it goes to seed and dries completely, the peel falls off and a network of tough fiber and black seeds are left. This fiber softens when wet but is strong enough to use for scrubbing and is wonderful for bathing. However, luffa is not well known as a summer vegetable. When it is cooked, it has a texture similar to okra—soft, smooth, and slippery. Because it is expensive, it is usually added to soups or cooked with other foods. It is a good complimentary vegetable, and it adds color and texture to a dish.

Butternut
Squash and
Buttercup Squash

南瓜
Nan Kua

The butternut squash has a taste similar to that of the Chinese pumpkin. It is readily available in the fall. The buttercup squash is starchier and sweeter than the butternut. It is not used with the same popularity as the butternut squash and the flavor is far superior to that of the pie pumpkin, so it is worth the effort to search for this squash. It is dark green, with a knob on the top like a brioche, and is about the size of a medium head of cabbage. It is sold in some farm stands.

Winter Melon

冬瓜
Tung Kua

Winter melon is actually a vegetable of the squash family. It has a hard dark green peel that is coated with a frost-like white powder. This melon is big so it is sold in wedges by weight. It will keep in the refrigerator for a long time if loosely covered with waxed paper (a tightly sealed plastic bag tends to promote quick rotting). When it is loosely wrapped, the outer layer may become dry. This dried-out part should be removed along with the peel before cooking.

Lotus Root

Ou

Ou is the rhizome of the lotus. Lotus is a plant whose rootstalks grow in the mud under water. Its leaves, blossoms, and seed pods are attached to long stems which are well above the water. *Ou* looks like short links of salami. Its flesh is ivory-colored and it has brown blotches on its skin. Inside there are long horizontal air channels. Depending on what area of China the plant comes from, a cross section of its rootstalk will show different numbers of holes, seven to eleven of them forming a circle around one small one, with even smaller holes situated at random around the large holes. *Ou* can be cooked as a vegetable or in soups. It may also be stuffed with glutinous rice and sweetened with sugar or honey, to serve as a dessert or a snack. It is an expensive ingredient and available only in large Chinese markets. It is most abundant in the fall.

Lotus Root Flour

Refer to "Grains, Flour, and Grain Products" (page 215).

Water Chestnuts

馬蹄 (荸薺)
Ma T'i

Water chestnuts are a corm of a plant that grows in the mud under several inches of water. It has the shape of a thick disk about one and a half inches in diameter and about three-fourths inch thick, with a sprout protruding at one of its flat sides and fine roots at the other side where the stem is attached. When the water chestnut is first dug out of the mud, it has a shiny dark red color, and it darkens when it dries out. Its raw flesh is porcelain white and the texture is much like that of raw potato. Its flavor, however, is sweet. But after cooking, unlike the potato, the water chestnut's texture remains crisp. Fresh water chestnuts are so superior in texture and taste to the canned ones that they cannot be compared. Peeling fresh water chestnuts is a difficult and time-consuming process, but they are well worth the effort. They can be candied like apples. Canned water chestnuts, which can be purchased in many supermarkets, retain the texture but not the flavor of the fresh ones. The fresh ones are available only in Chinese markets. Fresh water chestnuts do not spoil as readily and can be refrigerated for a long time.

Powdered Water Chestnuts

Refer to "Grains, Flours and Grain Products" (page 215).

Arrowhead

茨菇

Tz'u Ku

Arrowhead comes from a plant that grows in the mud in shallow stagnant ponds. Its leaves are shaped like arrowheads. The edible part is the starchy tuber that grows in the mud. The oval-shaped tuber is the size of a small onion and has root projections on one side and root fiber on the other. Its skin is white with two lines encircling the tuber where the sheathing leaves grew. The Chinese eat arrowhead as one would eat a potato; its texture is similar but the flavor is slightly different. It can be cooked in a dish as a starchy vegetable, or cut into thin slices and deep fried, like potato chips. It should be stored as one would store potatoes. It is available in Chinese markets seasonally.

Taros

芋艿

Yu Nai

Taro is the tuber of a plant with large green leaves sometimes called elephant ears. From the edible starchy main stalk, which is about eight inches long and four inches in diameter, grow the leaves and many smaller tubers the size of baking potatoes. That is why one often sees two sizes of taros in one basket—a few large ones and many smaller ones. When cooked, taros have a very smooth texture—almost slippery. It is used as a starchy vegetable and, when cooked in brown sugar syrup, as a snack. Boiled taros can be mashed and shaped into shells to wrap salty or sweet fillings. Taros have dark brown, almost black, fuzzy skins. When they are very fresh, the sprouting ends are pink. Taro also is marketed as flakes, like instant mashed potatoes. Both the dried flakes and fresh taros are available most of the time in Chinese markets. They should be stored in the same manner as potatoes.

Yams

山藥
Shan Yao

There are about ten species of yams that provide important nourishment all over the world. South Americans and Puerto Ricans eat one kind of yam known as yucca. *Shan yao* has a brown skin and white flesh. Unlike the kind of yam that is served with American Thanksgiving Dinner, the Chinese yam has rounded ends, like the large head of a toy baseball bat. Depending on growing conditions it can reach a length of twenty inches or more. *Shan yao* can be cooked in congee or sugar-spun or mashed into a more sophisticated sweet dish to serve at a banquet. It has a rather bland taste. The imported *shan yao* is very expensive; a pound of these yams may cost more than four pounds of bok choy. It is sold in large Chinese and Japanese markets.

Lily Bulbs

百合
Pai Ho

Lily bulbs are the bulbs of the garden lily. The bulb looks like a lotus blossom with double petals. It is ivory in color and sometimes is tinged pink at the tip of each petal. When it is fresh it cooks easily, but will fall apart when overcooked. It is usually used in sweet soups and served at special occasions, such as weddings, although when it is in season it is also eaten as a snack. Fresh lily bulbs are sold by weight with their petals intact. Dried ones, however, are sold as loose petals and are usually packed in plastic bags. If properly wrapped, lily bulbs can be kept in the refrigerator for many months. Lily bulbs are available in large Chinese markets, fresh ones only in season and dried ones most of the year.

Mushrooms

Although all mushrooms are fungi, for the purposes of Chinese cooking they are differentiated into those that have gills (mushrooms) and those that have no gills (fungi). Fresh mushrooms and fungi are sold locally, but after they have been dried they are sold all over the world. Several varieties of both mushrooms and fungi can be found in the Chinatowns of large cities. Dried mushrooms are marketed in several grades. They can be stored indefinitely if kept dry or in the freezer.

Dried, or Black, Mushrooms

香菌
Hsian Chun

This most popular type of mushroom is used, for its flavor, in many dishes as a complementary vegetable. Soaking the mushrooms in water for thirty minutes will bring the mushrooms back to their original shapes.

Winter Mushrooms

冬菇
Tung Ku

This is a thicker variety of black mushroom that, after soaking, is more tender then the dried, or black, mushroom. They are also more expensive and have a better flavor and aroma. These mushrooms need at least one to two hours to redevelop.

Straw
Mushrooms

草菇
Ts'ao Ku

Straw mushrooms have a completely different texture and flavor. Their caps are pointed, as opposed to the disk-shaped ones of the dried or black and winter mushrooms. They are marketed canned or dried.

Mouth
Mushrooms

口蘑
K'ou Mo

The mouth mushroom comes from the north of China. It has the strongest flavor of all the mushrooms used in Chinese cooking. It is marketed only in the dried form and its soaking water makes a delicious vegetarian soup stock. The mouth mushroom is a very expensive ingredient and is considered a delicacy. It is not easily available; occasionally it can be found in large markets of the Chinatowns of big cities.

Fresh, or White,
Mushrooms

鮮菇
Hsien Ku

This term is used in recipes for those fresh mushrooms available in all supermarkets. They may be used instead of black mushrooms, but they have an entirely different flavor and their taste will not be a good substitute in a given recipe.

Tree Ears
(Cloud Ears, or
Black Fungus)

木耳 (雲耳)
Mu Erh or Yün Erh

Tree ears are also called cloud ears. In a dried state they have the nondescript appearance of dark brown plastic chips. They vary in color from dark brown to gray to black. When redeveloped—if they are of good quality—they have the shape of the petals of double petunias. Those with very thick petals and pale color are not suitable for the recipes in this book. The flavor, though mild, can be compared to nothing in American cookery, so it is best to taste them.

Delicacies

Silver ears and bird's nests, both delicacies, are considered tonics for maintaining one's health. When they are properly prepared they are easily digestible. They are often given to elderly people. These two ingredients are packaged in fancy wrappings and sold for prized gifts.

Silver Ears
(White Fungus)

白木耳
Pai Mu Erh

The shape of a silver ear is similar to that of a tree ear but it is white and has a different flavor. It is also more expensive. Silver ears are added to both salty and sweet dishes and soups, while the black tree ears are never used in sweet dishes. If they are kept in a dry place they will not spoil. Silver ears are available in Chinese markets.

Bird's Nests

燕窩
Yen Wo

Swiflets in the South Pacific areas construct edible bird's nests by eating seaweed. The main component of the bird's nest is predigested protein, a glutinous secretion from the swiflet's salivary gland. The nests are built on seaside cliffs and cave walls. They have an interesting texture but do not have much taste. A good bird's nest soup needs a good soup stock. Bird's nests are sold in Chinese markets in several forms. They may be kept at room temperature and freezing will not affect them.

Bamboo Shoots

In China, bamboo shoots are either cooked alone as a vegetable or in other dishes to make them more interesting. In America, they are usually used as a complementary vegetable. Fresh bamboo shoots became available only recently. Over the last two winters, fresh winter bamboo shoots have been found occasionally in large Chinese markets in New York City's Chinatown. Bamboo shoots are best eaten fresh. Once canned, they lose much of their flavor. Some of the texture remains, however, and the crispy consistency can still be enjoyed. If canned bamboo shoots are not used up at once, they can be stored in the refrigerator for a long time; keep them submerged in a tightly covered jar completely filled with water. Shoots grown from different varieties of bamboo stalks differ subtly in their tastes, textures, and sizes, and they grow in different seasons. Bamboo shoots are like asparagus: the tips are more tender and the stalks become tougher toward the base. Cans of bamboo shoots contain both tender and tough parts. With proper cutting, both parts can be put to good use without waste. The tender parts can be cut into chunks using the roll-cut method, and the tougher parts can be cut into julienne strips of small dice.

Winter Bamboo Shoots

冬 筍
Tung Sun

In the winter, when the shoots first begin to grow, they are collected by digging underground. That is why these shoots are called winter bamboo shoots. They are relatively small in size and have the best taste of all bamboo shoots. They have a smooth beige-colored shell and, when peeled, are about the size of medium pine cones.

Spring Bamboo Shoots

毛 筍
Mao Sun

Spring shoots grow straight up from the ground. They are the largest of all bamboo shoots and sometimes they may reach several feet in height and three or four inches in diameter. The shells are dark brown, fuzzy, and have a sheen. Hence, spring shoots are called hair bamboo shoots.

Summer Bamboo Shoots

竹 筍
Chu Sun

In the summer there is a smaller species of bamboo shoots that grows to the size of thin asparagus. These are called "bamboo" bamboo shoots in Chinese. Flat-tip bamboo shoots are cut from these shoots.

Braised Bamboo
Shoots

油燜筍
Yu Men Sun

Canned braised bamboo shoots are seasoned and can be eaten right out of the can without further preparation. They are a good item to serve as hors d'oeuvres.

Flat-Tip
Bamboo Shoots

扁尖筍
Pien Chien Sun

The name of this ingredient is misleading. These bamboo shoots are cut from *chu sun,* the thin summer bamboo shoots. Only the tender tips are used; thus they are called flat-tip bamboo shoots. They are preserved mainly with salt, then dried. These shoots have a distinct flavor and are often added to soups. In China, flat-tip bamboo shoots are packed in loosely woven bamboo baskets lined with bamboo leaves. But in America a basketful is too large a quantity to be sold, so it is divided into small portions and packed in plastic bags to be sold by weight. It can be stored in the refrigerator in a plastic bag or in a non-metallic container for at least one year.

Tender Shells of
Bamboo Shoots

筍衣
Sun Yi

The tender shells at the tips of bamboo shoots are edible before they mature and darken in color. When peeling fresh bamboo shoots, the tender shells are left on to be eaten. Sometimes these shells are taken off and preserved separately by parboiling and drying. Dried *sun yi* cannot often be found, but occasionally one finds them packaged in plastic bags in large Chinese grocery stores.

Sour Tender
Bamboo Shoot
Shells

酸筍衣
Suan Sun Yi

The Cantonese like sour tender bamboo shells. They are packed in water with salt and with or without vinegar in cans. They make any dish more interesting.

Bamboo Leaves

粽箬
Tsung Je

粽子
Tsung Tzu

There is one kind of bamboo that grows no taller than three feet and has leaves that are about eighteen inches long and three to four inches wide. These leaves are collected to wrap glutinous rice with sweet or salty fillings. The leaves give a good flavor. The wrapped rice is called *tsung tzu.* Although it is eaten all year, this food is especially prepared to be eaten on the fifth day of the fifth month during the dragon festival. Shops sell it as a cooked food. Bamboo leaves can be found in large markets of Chinatowns, dried and tied in stacks. Dried bamboo leaves are very brittle and if cracked are difficult to handle. They can be kept indefinitely, and will not spoil nor lose their fragrance.

Preserved Foods

Before canning and freezing were developed, the Chinese preserved foods by several methods. They prevented unseasoned foods from spoiling by blanching and thoroughly drying; another method was salting—first removing most of the liquid from vegetables, then seasoning them with spices for added flavors. Both methods created interesting tastes and textures. All preserved foods have strong flavors. The unseasoned and dried foods are used as ingredients in dishes; the salted and spiced foods are used for seasoning bland foods.

Seasoned Preserved Foods

Chinese Celery Cabbage

冬 菜
Tung Ts'ai

Chinese celery cabbage is preserved in both Szechuan and Tientsin. Both the leaves and stems are cut into small bits. In Tientsin it is preserved with salt, garlic, and other spices; in Szechuan it is prepared without garlic. The color is light brown. It is packed very tightly in earthenware, cans, or glass jars, and can be found in Chinese markets.

Szechuan Preserved Vegetable

四川榨菜
Szechuan Cha Ts'ai

Cha ts'ai is a specialty of the Szechuan province. It is made from a special variety of the mustard green that has stems with many knobs. Only the stems are used. It is preserved in salt along with minced hot chili pepper. It comes either chopped or in chunks and is packed into jars or cans. If it tastes too peppery, wash out some of the hot chili flavor before cooking. This vegetable is available in Oriental food shops and Chinese markets.

Yunnan Pickled Turnips

雲南大頭菜
Yunnan Ta T'ou Ts'ai

The province of Yunnan is famous for its pickled turnips. Only the root of the vegetable is used. It is cut into chunks, preserved in salt and soy sauce, then sun-dried. Its color is dark brown or almost black. It is packed in glass jars or plastic bags and sold in Chinese markets.

Red-in-Snow

雪裡蕻
Hsüeh Li Hung

People of Chekiang and Kiangsu preserve a delicious pickled vegetable that is called "red-in-snow." It is a leafy green much like the top of a turnip. Both the leaves and stems are preserved. It is grown in the United States and can be bought fresh in Chinese markets. Only the tender parts of this vegetable are eaten fresh. To be preserved, the vegetable must be salted several days before it is ready to be eaten. Red-in-snow comes in 7-ounce cans and is cut up in 2- to 3-inch sections. The best brand is *Ma-Ling,* produced in Shanghai.

Fermented Red-in-Snow

霉乾菜

Mei Ken Ts'ai

Fermented red-in-snow is made by piling the fresh red-in-snow in a heap and letting it sit a few days until it turns partially yellow. Then it is washed and hung up to dry. When partially dried out, the vegetable is salted. It is then thoroughly dried in the sun and turns dark brown. Sometimes bits of bamboo shoots are added to the vegetable. After red-in-snow has gone through this long preserving process it develops a special fragrance. It is said that when any food is cooked with fermented red-in-snow it will not spoil. Hence, it is often used in the summer.

Cantonese Preserved Vegetable

廣東冲菜

Canton Ch'ung Ts'ai

The Cantonese usually use this vegetable, which is made from a turnip with the top intact. Equal portions of stems and vertically sliced leaves and roots are tied together with one of the tougher stems into a bundle the size of a large walnut. One little bundle is more than enough to season an average serving of soup. Moist at first, the *ch'ung ts'ai* ball is covered with salt crystals when it dries. It is very salty, and will not spoil if it is kept in the refrigerator. It is sold in Chinatown packed in plastic bags.

Sour Mustard Greens

酸菜

Suan Ts'ai

To pickle mustard greens, the Cantonese parboil the whole plant, stems and leaves uncut, and put it into brine. It is left to ferment until it has just begun to sour. It is then ready to be eaten. Sour mustard greens are sold packed in jars or in open vats, soaking in the original brine. They can be found in some Oriental food shops and in Chinese markets. If the vegetable is too sour, it can be rinsed with cold water before cooking.

Dried Salted White Turnips

蘿蔔乾

Lo Po Kan

The white turnip is preserved all over China. It is also very popular in Japan. It is the least expensive vegetable. It is so salty that a little bit will go a long way. The turnip is salted and sun dried; sugar, hot pepper, and other spices may be added. It can be cut into small bits or long strips. It comes in cans and glass jars of various sizes, and in plastic bags. Some salted turnips are spiced with hot peppers and are ready to eat, while others have to be cooked with other foods. They are available in Chinese markets.

Preserved
Cucumbers

醬瓜
Chiang Kua

Cucumbers are pickled all over China. They are preserved in various stages of growth. Some are pickled before the blossoms have had a chance to open and others are pickled in various stages up to full maturity. The most common pickled cucumbers are made from fully grown ones. They are cut into strips, one-half inch wide and about two inches long, and preserved in soy sauce. They are packed in 6-ounce cans and can be found in Chinese grocery shops. Once a can of pickled cucumbers is opened, it should be transferred to a rustproof covered jar and stored in the refrigerator. It will not spoil.

Tea Cucumbers

茶瓜
Ch'a Kua

The Cantonese tea cucumber is similar to preserved cucumbers. However, it contains sugar and is less salty. It comes in cans of various sizes and it has to be stored in the same manner as regular preserved cucumbers.

Flat-Tip
Bamboo Shoots

Refer to page 203.

Sour Tender
Bamboo Shells

Refer to page 203.

**Unseasoned
Dried Vegetables**

Dried Bok Choy

菜乾
Ts'ai Kan

Bok choy may be preserved by drying after it is parboiled, without adding seasonings. Since it is not salty, it can be used in large amounts; often it is used as the main ingredient for fillings. It is also used in soups.

Dried Bamboo
Shoots

筍乾
Sun Kan

Bamboo shoots can be preserved in the same manner as bok choy. But it is used only as a complementary vegetable in a dish.

Day Lily Buds
(Golden Needles)

金針
Chin Chen

Lily buds are dried and used as a complementary vegetable. They are often used in combination with tree ears. To use, soak them in boiling water for about ten minutes and then remove the hard stems. The water used for soaking is generally discarded.

Seaweeds	Seaweeds are cooked with other foods, mixed in salads, or added to desserts to give interesting flavors and textures. They are sold dried and should be kept away from moisture in tightly covered glass jars. They do not need refrigeration. They are available in large Chinese grocery shops and are sold in small quantities, packed in plastic bags.
Green Seaweed 苔條 *T'ai T'iao*	This mosslike seaweed comes dried in wads or as matted chips. When fried in oil it has a toasted fragrance and a slight iodine taste. It is used to flavor foods and it comes either unseasoned or salted.
Hair Seaweed 髮菜 *Fa Ts'ai*	Hair seaweed derives its name from its appearance. It is dark purple or almost black and looks like intertwined strands of hair. It has very little flavor but gives an interesting texture to dishes.
Sea Girdle (Kelp) 海帶 *Hai Tai*	This dark green-brown ribbonlike seaweed is about 3 to 4 inches wide and may grow as long as one hundred feet. It is sold in Oriental food stores wrapped in cellophane packages. It comes dried and either finely shredded or cut into sections 6 to 8 inches long. After being reconstituted it is cut into small pieces and cooked in soups or with other foods. Shredded kelp is served uncooked as a salad. Dry kelp can be kept indefinitely, but once reconstituted it should be soaked in water until it is used and may be kept in the refrigerator up to a week.
Laver 紫菜 *Tze Ts'ai*	Laver is a delicate-looking veillike seaweed. It comes in different shades of red and purple. The one most commonly eaten is purple. As the Chinese like to name foods by colors, it is simply called "the purple vegetable." Dried laver comes in thin 8 x 8-inch sheets in stacks of eight to ten, folded in half, and wrapped in cellophane. Laver is never cooked; to serve it, just drop small pieces into hot soup. Laver contains iodine, which gives the soup a special flavor.
Agar-Agar 洋菜 *Yang Ts'ai*	Agar-agar is a gelatinous substance obtained from seaweed (moss). It comes in powder form, in long solid rectangular sections, or in fine strips. The powdered and solid forms are used to make desserts. The fine strips are used for salads. Only cold water should be used to soften agar-agar, for it will melt in hot water. One Japanese company markets powdered agar-agar premeasured and packaged in a convenient portion of 2 tablespoons. The other forms of agar-agar are wrapped in plastic bags and sold by weight.

SOYBEANS, SOYBEAN PRODUCTS, AND LEGUMES

Fresh Young
Soybeans

毛豆
Mao Tou

Fresh young soybeans are delicious to eat. They are in season in the early fall and are available in Chinese markets. They come in dark, fuzzy pods and are sold by weight. Young soybeans are like corn and should be eaten as soon as they are picked from the plant. They may be cooked with or without pods.

Dried Soybeans

黄豆
Huang Tou

Dried soybeans are about the size of dried peas and are yellow in color. Packed in one-pound quantities in plastic bags, they are sold in many Oriental food shops and in health food stores.

Soybean Sprouts

黄豆芽
Huang Tou Ya

Soybean sprouts are sold by weight in Chinese markets. The best bean sprouts are available in cooler weather. When bought fresh, they will keep in the refrigerator for 2 to 3 days, or longer if they are kept in a brown paper bag placed inside a plastic bag. Mung bean sprouts are discussed on page 92.

Soy Sauce

Refer to "Condiments and Seasonings" (page 219).

Salted Black
Beans

Refer to "Condiments and Seasonings" (page 220).

Brown Bean
Sauce

Refer to "Condiments and Seasonings" (page 220).

Ground Brown
Bean Sauce

Refer to "Condiments and Seasonings" (page 220).

Hoisin Sauce

Refer to "Condiments and Seasonings" (page 221).

Soybean Milk

豆漿
Tou Chiang

Soybean milk is extracted from soaked soybeans ground with water and strained through cloth. The straining removes the husk and most of the solid residue from the beans. The white liquid obtained is the bean milk, which contains most of the protein. Bean milk must be brought to a boil to get rid of the strong bean flavor. It is usually served hot as a beverage with breakfast. It should be stored in the same manner as regular milk.

Soybean Milk Skin

When soybean milk is boiled, a film forms on top of the liquid, very much as with regular milk. This film is lifted off the boiling bean milk and dried. The skin of the bean milk is called by many names. Each region has a different name for it, as does each food processor, and the thickness, shape, and wrapping may be different. There are four kinds of dried bean milk skin readily available in Chinese food shops. They need not be refrigerated. They should be used within two months from the date of purchase. Since they contain oil, they can turn rancid.

二 竹
Erh Chu

Erh Chu is a type of soybean milk skin that is cut into rectangles 1½ x 4 inches and ⅛ inch thick. The pieces come stacked and wrapped in paper, in half- or one-pound packages.

圓 竹
Yüan Chu

This bean milk skin comes in sticks. Once reconstituted, its thickness is about the same as *erh chu*. It comes in half- or one-pound paper-wrapped packages.

三 邊 腐竹
San Pien Fu Chu

This bean milk is half-moon-shaped. When it is still soft it is folded into 6 x 10-inch rectangles, then dried. It is thinner than *erh chu*. It is wrapped in half- or one-pound packages.

腐衣 (腐皮)
Fu Yi

Fu yi is the thinnest of the bean milk skins. It is paper-thin and almost transparent. When dried it is very brittle, and it must be handled very gently. It is used mainly to wrap fillings. It comes in stacks of eight to ten sheets which are wrapped in paper and look like large flat bags. In shops it is usually hung high on a hook, to prevent rough handling by customers. A frozen *fu yi* that is only partially dried is still pliable and is shipped from Taiwan. It has to be kept in the refrigerator or freezer, as it tends to become moldy.

Soybean Milk Residue

豆 腐 渣
Tou Fu Cha

The residue obtained from the soaked ground soybeans after the milk is removed can be cooked into a delicious dish. What is not used for food is made into a feed for animals or put into the ground as fertilizer.

Curdled Soybean Milk

豆 腐 花
Tou Fu Hua

When a coagulant is added to boiled soybean milk, it curdles. Curdled soybean milk is the most tender form of bean curd. It is eaten hot with soy sauce or cold with syrup as a snack. Curdled bean milk is sold only in bean curd factories by the pint.

Bean Curd
Coagulant

熟石膏
Shou Shih Kao

Shou shih kao is a white substance which comes in powder form. It is used to coagulate soybean milk to make *tou fu* (bean curd). *Shou shih kao* consists of chemicals which can be easily found in China. But in the United States, it is only sold in a few specialty shops in Chinatowns of large cities. *Tou fu*, like cheese, is seldom made at home. It is easier to find *tou fu* ready-made then the *shou shih kao*.

Tender Soybean
Curd

嫩豆腐
Nen Tou Fu

When some water is removed from the curdled bean milk, it is known as fresh tender bean curd. It is cut into squares 4 x 4 x 1½ inches.

Firm Soybean
Curd

老豆腐
Lao Tou Fu

When a coagulant is added to the boiled bean milk of a different concentration and some of the water is removed, the milk becomes firm bean curd. It is firmer than the tender bean curd and is cut into 3 x 3 x ¾-inch squares.

Soybean Curd in
Sealed Container

Both the firm and tender soybean curd come in sealed, water-filled plastic containers. A preservative is added to the water and they can be kept in the refrigerator for up to a month.

Storing Soybean
Curd

The size of bean curd squares may vary, depending upon the processors, who set their own standards. Bean curd is more readily available than other bean milk products. Both tender and firm bean curds can be purchased in Oriental food shops and in some big supermarkets. They are sold prepackaged in sealed plastic containers or loose by the square. Bean curd spoils easily, so extra care should be given when transporting it from the grocery in hot weather and in storing it. Loose pieces of fresh bean curd should be placed in a container and submerged in water. If the water is changed every two days, it can be kept at least one week. If it is kept in a tightly sealed container filled all the way to the top with water and as little air as possible is allowed to remain in the container, bean curd can be kept at least ten days without changing the water. The growth of bacteria will spoil bean curd. Since bacteria need air to grow and there is little air in the container, such growth is deterred. If a preservative is added to the water, it will keep the bean curd fresh even longer. However the bean curd is stored, the container should be placed in the coldest area of the refrigerator, but not the freezer. Always rinse bean curd with running water before using.

Pressed Bean Curd Sheet

百葉
Pai Yeh

Fresh bean curd sheet looks almost like a piece of unbleached muslin. When it is frozen, the color turns darker, to a light brown. It is made into square sheets of various sizes. It is used to wrap fillings and it is also sometimes cut into short strips and cooked in dishes along with seasoning vegetables. Pressed bean curd sheet is best eaten fresh but frozen ones are also good. Pressed bean curd sheets come from Taiwan, and are wrapped in stacks of 8 to 10 sheets and come in sealed 8-ounce plastic bags. Occasionally fresh *pai yeh* made by local merchants is available. If it is properly wrapped it will keep for a long time. The frozen pressed bean curd sheets are available only in large Chinese markets.

Pressed Soybean Curd

豆腐乾
Tou Fu Kan
Plain

白豆腐乾
Pai Tou Fu Kan
Seasoned

五香豆腐乾
Wu Hsiang Tou Fu Kan

When even more water is pressed out of firm bean curd, it becomes pressed bean curd. Its texture becomes much firmer than that of regular bean curd and it is almost like a firm cheese. Pressed bean curd may be bought either plain or seasoned. The plain curd is white. The seasoned curd is cooked in soy sauce with star anise, giving it a brown color. The two types are available in most Chinese grocery stores and in some Oriental food shops. They should be stored submerged in liquid. The white pressed bean curd should be soaked in salt water (made of 1 tablespoon salt to 4 cups water) in a covered container. The seasoned pressed bean curd should be soaked in salt water and soy sauce. If stored in the coldest part of the refrigerator, they will keep for several weeks.

Fried Soybean Curd

油豆腐
Yu Tou Fu

The name is self-explanatory. The bean curd is cut into 1½-inch cubes and deep fried in oil until a golden yellow crust forms outside, while the inside of the bean curd remains soft. Fried soybean curd is sold by weight, usually in half- or one-pound plastic bags. Approximately twenty medium-fried bean curd cubes will weigh one pound. This curd can be kept in the refrigerator for two to three days and may also be frozen.

Fermented Soybean Curd

腐乳(紅.白)
Fu-Ju

Fu-Ju is fermented soybean curd, soaked in a solution of salt, spices, wine, and water. It comes in two colors, white and red, which have slightly different tastes. It has the texture of very soft cheese but is much saltier. Fu-ju can be used to flavor vegetables and meats in cooking, or it can be served right from the jar or can. When served alone, a small amount is usually placed on a small dish and eaten with congee. Once a can of fu-ju is opened, it should be transferred to a jar with a rustproof cap. The process of fermentation does not stop; the longer the fu-ju is kept, the softer it will be. But if it is kept in the refrigerator, it will not spoil.

Mung Beans

綠豆

Lu Tou

Three very important food items are made from the mung bean: bean sprouts, cellophane noodles, and mung bean sheets.

Mung Bean Sprouts

綠豆芽

Lu Tou Ya

Mung bean sprouts are one of the most popular Chinese vegetables in the United States. They can be found in almost every large city supermarket. If they are very fresh and are kept away from excess moisture, they can be stored in the refrigerator for two to three days.

Cellophane Noodles

粉絲

Fen Sze

Mung Bean Sheets

粉皮

Fen P'i

When mung beans are soaked, ground, and strained, a translucent liquid is obtained. The liquid is then made into noodles and round sheets. Both the noodles and sheets are opaque when cool and transparent when warm. This transparent quality is the reason the noodles are called cellophane noodles. They are sold in a dried form. The noodles are tied into bundles weighing two ounces, half a pound, or one pound. The mung bean sheets are sold in stacks of eight to ten sheets, packed in plastic bags.

Dried Fava Beans

蠶豆

Ts'an Tou

Sprouted Fava Beans

發芽豆

Fa Ya Tou

When young, fava beans can be eaten as a vegetable. When dried, they can be germinated. Unlike the other two kinds of bean sprouts, the sprouted fava bean has a much larger bean and shorter sprout. The dried beans can be stored easily and reconstituted any time they are needed. Soaked beans can be pureed and used as a starchy vegetable. They can also be deep fried and seasoned to eat as a snack, like peanuts. Dried fava beans give flavor to soups and also are an important ingredient in making brown bean sauce in place of soybeans. Fava beans are not used as often as soybeans because they are more expensive, but they make a better and sweeter bean sauce.

Yard-Long Beans or Pole Beans

長豇豆

Ch'ang Chiang Tou

Home gardeners often grow these long beans out of curiosity. Some seed growers claim their seeds will produce beans as long as three feet. Hence, they are called yard-long beans. The beans that are sold in the Chinese markets, in bunches or by weight, are about twelve to fourteen inches long. The pods are not as fleshy as those of green beans, but after they are cooked, they have a fine texture and unique flavor.

Red Beans

紅豆
Hung Tou

Red beans are used most often in sweet pastries in the form of a paste. In the relatively few sweet dishes in Chinese cookery, red beans play an important role. Red beans are sold by weight in plastic bags and can be found in many Oriental food stores. The paste can be made at home or bought in cans.

Salted Black Beans

Refer to "Condiments and Seasonings" (page 220).

SEEDS, NUTS, FRUITS, AND EGGS

Sesame Seeds

芝蔴(白.黑)
Chih Ma

Sesame seeds may be black or white and are slightly larger than poppy seeds. They are often used for their flavor. When toasted, they have a special fragrance. These seeds can be ground to make a paste or to obtain oil. In southeastern China they are used mostly in sweet foods. Like the Italians, the Chinese also top their pastries with these seeds. Raw sesame seeds can be bought in Italian and Chinese groceries.

Sesame Paste

Refer to "Condiments and Seasonings" (page 221).

Sesame Oil

Refer to "Condiments and Seasonings" (page 221).

Lotus Seeds

蓮心
Lien Hsin

The lotus seed pod resembles the nozzle of a watering can. The seeds sit in a well formed oval cavity lined with a green smooth peel, and there is soft white fiber padded under the peel. When young, the seeds are green; they turn brown when mature. They are used mostly in desserts or sweet soups. They are definitely a delicacy and are expensive, but the flavor and texture make the expense worthwhile. They come ready for use, sold by half-and one-pound units in plastic bags. They can be found in large Chinese grocery stores. It is best to use the seeds as soon as possible, although they will not spoil; aging, however, tends to affect their delicate texture.

Chestnuts

栗子
Li Tzu

Fresh chestnuts are at their best around Thanksgiving time. They have a tendency to mold easily if kept in plastic bags, but a brown paper bag is porous enough to prevent them from spoiling. Dried chestnuts are available all year and can be bought in Chinese and Italian markets. They should be soaked in cold water before being cooked. It is important to cull the chestnuts so that any spoiled parts are removed. Inclusion of a few spoiled chestnuts can ruin all the effort that goes into a delicious dish.

Ginkgo Nuts

白菓

Pai Kuo

The ginkgo is the edible pit of an inedible fruit. The ginkgo tree thrives in urban surroundings and is frequently used as a sidewalk shade tree. The pit (or nut) of the fruit is white and shaped like a tiny football, about the size of a large jelly bean. The fresh meat of the nut is chartreuse and becomes translucent when cooked. The nuts are never eaten raw. Ginkgo nuts are available canned, shelled, or loose in their shells and are sold by the pound.

Jujubes (Red Dates)

紅棗

Hung Tsao

Jujubes come from the northern part of China. When fresh, they have a green color. They are crisp and sweet. They are usually available dried and have dark red crinkled skins. Sizes vary from that of seedless grapes to that of large olives. They are sold in Chinese markets in plastic bags, and are best stored in the refrigerator or freezer.

Litchi

荔枝

Li Chih

A fruit often mentioned in history books, litchi was sent from Canton to the court at Peking for the Emperor in pony express style. It is a subtropical fruit that grows in clusters on tall trees. It has the shape and size of a strawberry, and its shell is thin, brittle, bumpy, and has a reddish-brown color. The fruit has a porcelain-white pulp and a large amount of sweet juice with a perfumed fragrance. It has a shiny dark brown pit of varying sizes; it can be as large as a small olive. In the United States, it is grown in abundance in Florida and Hawaii. Fresh litchi are not readily available in the North because they spoil easily. It is in season in June, when it is sold in Chinese markets. The dried fruit is sometimes called litchi nut. Canned litchi can be bought all year round.

Longan or Dragon's Eyes

龍眼(桂圓)

Lung Yen

Dragon's eyes are the same type of fruit as the litchi except that the shell is smooth and the dried ones are covered with a cinnamon-colored powder. They are smaller than the litchi, and have an entirely different taste. They come dried, canned, or pitted, and are packed tightly into four-ounce packages. They are used for cooking in sweet soups or served as a fruit dessert. They can be bought in Chinese markets.

Loquats

枇杷

P'i Pa

A loquat is a fruit with a fuzzy peel and comes from a tree with fuzzy leaves and fuzzy stems. It is round or oval-shaped, about the size of a walnut, and grows in clusters. Loquats have large brown shiny pits. Usually one to four pits are in each fruit, grown together like a miniature puzzle ball. The fruit is juicy and sweet with a delicate flavor. Its color may be white or apricot. Those who never have seen a loquat may find it interesting, but as a fruit it is not valuable because it has more pits than flesh. Fresh loquats are seldom found in markets, but canned ones are more readily available. Canned loquats are used in desserts to add color and texture. In California and Florida, loquat trees are planted to add to landscapes. Enormous loquat trees can be found at Stanford University, where they are used as shade trees.

Salted Duck Eggs

鹹蛋
Hsien Tan

Salted eggs are duck eggs preserved in brine. The salt penetrates the shells and makes the eggs salty. Salted eggs must be cooked before they can be eaten.

Thousand-Year Eggs

皮蛋
P'i Tan

Thousand-year eggs are preserved in an alkaline mud mixture. The chemical penetrates the eggshell, turning both the white and yolk a dark brownish-green color. The egg is eaten uncooked. Before cracking the egg shell, all the mud must be removed, then the egg is thoroughly cleaned. Once it is cleaned, it is cut lengthwise into wedges and put on a plate to be served with soy sauce. It is sometimes garnished with gingerroot strips. The preservative coating of the eggs dries up easily in dry weather and in the refrigerator. The eggs should thus be kept in tightly sealed plastic bags.

Quail Eggs

鵪鶉蛋
An Chu'un Tan

Quail eggs come in cans and are already hard-boiled. They are available in Chinese markets and in delicacy shops.

GRAINS, FLOUR, AND GRAIN PRODUCTS

Rice

Rice, like wheat, has different varieties with different qualities. For consumers it is classified by the length of the kernel and the degree of gluten. Long-grain rice is the fluffiest. In China it used to be more expensive because, when cooked, it yielded more volume per cup than the short-grain rice. Short- or oval-grain rice is stickier when cooked. One's preference for rice depends on the region of origin and what one is accustomed to. Glutinous rice is often added to regular rice to make congee. Most of the time, however, it is used for stuffings, shells to wrap fillings, sweet dishes, and special foods, such as *tsung tzu*. Brown rice is unpolished rice with some of the bran left on the kernel. It is more nutritious.

Wine Rice

酒釀
Chiu Niang

Wine rice is fermented rice. It can be made at home using wine yeast, which is available in Chinese markets and herb shops. Wine yeast comes in walnut-sized balls and is a fermenting agent. Ready-made wine rice comes in glass jars, soaked in its own sweet liquid. It can often be found in large Chinese markets. Wine rice must be stored in the refrigerator.

Rice Wine

黄酒
Huang Chiu

Shaohsing rice wine is the best and most popular Chinese wine. It can be purchased in some wine stores. If it is not available, use dry sherry instead.

Flour Products

The starch from different plants is ground into flour and can then be made into many delicious foods. The flours do not have distinct flavor. When made into dough and cooked, they all have different consistencies and characteristics. With the exception of water chestnut flour, which comes in smaller packages, all these flours are packed in brightly printed paper wrappers covered with cellophane, in one-pound units. They are available in Chinese grocery stores and in some Oriental food shops. They may be stored as one would store ordinary wheat flour, and if stored in the freezer, they will keep indefinitely.

Rice Flour

粘米粉
Chan Mi Fen

Rice flour is ground from long-grain rice. It is used for making cakes and shells to wrap either sweet or salty fillings. Very often it is mixed with glutinous rice flour to obtain the desired texture.

Glutinous, or
Sweet Rice,
Flour

糯米粉
No Mi Fen

Sweet rice flour is ground from glutinous rice. It is used in the same way as long-grain rice flour, though they are not interchangeable. Sweet rice flour has a softer and stickier texture than plain rice flour. Japanese sweet rice flour is less glutinous than that of the Chinese.

Water-Ground
Rice Flour

水磨粉
Shui Mo Fen

Rice ground with water is another method of making rice flour. The long-grain or the glutinous rice kernels are soaked in water and ground while wet. Afterward the excess water is squeezed out. This method produces a finer texture than the dry-ground flours. Because of easy spoilage, the rice is sold only during cool weather in lumps by weight. It is used in the same manner as the dry rice flours. Less liquid is used when mixing the dough. These flours must be kept in the refrigerator for two or three days, or they may be frozen for longer periods. The water-ground flours are sold in Chinese bean curd shops.

Lotus Root
Flour

藕 粉
Ou Fen

Lotus root flour is similar to arrowroot flour. After the lotus root stalk is crushed, the starch is washed out and allowed to settle and the water is drained off; what remains is *ou fen*. Like arrowroot flour, it consists mostly of a very digestible starch. It is used to make soft paste to feed infants as a milk supplement. Western doctors who practice in China often prescribe *ou fen* gruel to patients with gastric ulcers. *Ou fen* gruel needs no cooking; just add boiling water and stir until it becomes smooth. It is eaten with a spoon as one would eat hot cereal. Lotus root flour looks like dark pink powder. It comes in a paper-wrapper package and can be found in large Chinese markets.

Water Chestnut
Flour

馬蹄粉
Ma T'i Fen

Water chestnut flour is used to make batter and to thicken sauces. It gives a very shiny glaze to cooked food. This flour is also used to make cakes. Only small amounts are used to thicken a sauce; therefore, half- or quarter-pound packages are available. Only large Chinese grocery stores carry this special flour.

Wheat Gluten

麵 筋
Mien Ching

Gluten is made of a dough of wheat flour mixed with water after the starch has been washed away. It can be made at home, but in China it never is, simply because it involves too many tedious steps. Gluten can be used in cooking when it is raw, fried, steamed, boiled, or canned.

Deep-Fried
Gluten

油 麵 筋
Yu Mien Ching

Yu mien ching is a specialty from Wus Hsi, a town about one hundred miles northwest of Shanghai. When a small piece of raw gluten is deep fried, it puffs up into a ball and is fried until it is golden brown. Usually the balls are about 1½ inches in diameter. They are packed in plastic bags and sold in Chinese markets. They should be stored in the refrigerator, where they will keep up to a week; they will keep longer in the freezer.

Fresh or Dried
Wheat Gluten

烤 麩
K'ao Fu

Fresh (steamed) wheat gluten comes from Taiwan as frozen chunks of irregular shapes, packed in plastic bags, and sold by weight in a few specialty shops in the China-towns of large cities. It can be stored in the freezer for a few months. Dried wheat gluten looks like pieces of cut-up dried bread. It has to be softened in water before using. It can be kept at room temperature for a long time. It is packaged in plastic bags and sold in large Chinese markets.

Canned Gluten

Several brands of canned gluten are available in the markets. They are prepared in both Taiwan and in the United States. Those canned in Taiwan, such as "mock abalone," are actually made from gluten. They are seasoned and can be eaten right out of the can. Canned gluten is a convenient ingredient to add to almost any dish. Here in the United States there are several companies who make meat substitutes out of both soy meal and wheat gluten. Some are flavored with spices and others with salt. Canned gluten, seasoned only with salt, is the most suitable for Chinese cooking. It may be found in health food stores or in large department stores. The cans come in different sizes.

Rice Cakes

寧波年糕

Ningpo Nien Kao

Rice cakes are a specialty of the seaport city of Ningpo. They are commonly called Ningpo rice cakes, and are made from a mixture of water-ground flours of long- and short-grain rices. They may be bought in Chinese markets in plastic bags containing stacks of eight to ten rectangles, 5 x 1½ x ½-inch. Since they do not contain salt, the rice cakes cannot be stored for long periods. They can be kept in the coldest part of the refrigerator for up to two months if they are sliced then submerged in water in a container with a watertight cover. *Ningpo nien kao* also come in dried slices. They can be kept at room temperature; before cooking, just soak them in cold water until they are soft.

Rice Noodles
(Rice Sticks)

米粉

Mi Fen

Rice noodles are made from rice flour. These noodles do not need to be parboiled. They need only to be soaked in water before cooking with other foods. Rice noodles can be stir-fried or dropped into soups. Overcooking turns them into a paste. They are available as dried rectangular wads, wrapped in paper in one-pound packages. Each package is divided into four wads, easily accessible serving portions. They are sold in Chinese groceries. There are several brands that are equally good.

Egg Noodles

蛋麵

Tan Mien

Egg noodles are sold fresh in Chinese groceries. They may be found in one-pound plastic bags in the refrigerated cases. Thicknesses vary, depending upon the manufacturer. Fresh egg noodles can be kept in the freezer. If frozen, the noodles should be cooked immediately. Just drop them in boiling water and stir until they thaw completely. Continue to boil until the desired tenderness is obtained.

Won Ton and
Shao Mai
Wrappers
餛飩皮
燒賣皮
Won Ton and
Shao Mai P'i

The thickness of won ton wrappers depends on the manufacturer. A one-pound package will include anywhere from 75 to 150 wrappers. Won ton wrappers are sold wrapped in waxed paper. *Shao mai* wrappers are very similar to won ton wrappers except that won ton wrappers are square and the latter are round. They come both fresh and frozen.

Canton Spring
Roll Wrappers
廣東春捲皮
*Kwang Tung
Ch'un Chüan P'i*

Regular egg roll wrappers are much like won ton wrappers. There are no standard sizes, but they are square, about 7 x 7 inches. They come wrapped in waxed paper in one-pound packages.

Shanghai Spring
Roll Wrappers
上海春捲皮
*Shang Hai Ch'un
Chüan P'i*

Shanghai spring roll wrappers are either square or round. The round ones resemble doilies about 7 inches in diameter. They are packed in plastic bags in stacks of ten to twenty pieces. All egg roll wrappers dry easily. When dry, they are very hard to handle and make wrapping almost impossible. As soon as they are brought home, the wrappers should be put into tightly sealed plastic bags and stored in the refrigerator or freezer. The wrappers freeze very well. If they should become too dry, wrap the *ch'un chüan p'i* in a damp cloth for a few hours before using. Won ton, *shao mai,* and Canton and Shanghai spring roll wrappers can be found in the refrigerated cases of may Oriental food shops.

CONDIMENTS AND SEASONINGS

Soy Sauce
醬油
Chiang Yu

Dark or Thick
Soy Sauce

老抽(深)
Lao Ch'ou

Soy sauce is the most important seasoning liquid in Chinese cooking and is often used in place of salt. There are many brands in various-size containers. Some makers produce two kinds of soy sauce, dark and light or thick and thin. Both light and dark soy sauce are good for cooking. The light one is preferred for dipping. Some people combine the sauces to suit their tastes. It is a good idea to try different brands until a suitable sauce is found. Always use the same brand so that an accurate degree of saltiness is obtained for every dish prepared. It can not be overemphasized that different brands of soy sauce have different concentrations of salt, and one should adjust the amounts used depending on the brand and one's individual taste.

Light or Thin
Soy Sauce

生抽（淺）
Sheng Ch'ou

The best cooks may forget that a dish may be either too salty or too bland because a different brand of soy sauce was used. Soy sauce comes not only in different shades but also flavors, such as mushroom soy sauce and, for nonvegetarians, shrimp roe soy sauce. Flavored soy sauces are used mainly for dips and for special flavors in salads, noodles, and as a final touch to a dish. Soy sauces for cooking are commonly found in many supermarkets that have Chinese food sections. If the soy sauce comes in a can, it should be transferred to a glass bottle once the can is opened. It can be kept at room temperature indefinitely.

Salted Black
Beans

豆豉
Tou Shih

Black beans preserved in salt are used to flavor bland foods, such as eggplant or bean curd. They come in small portions packed in plastic bags, cans, and jars. The beans are sold in Chinese markets. They can be stored in the refrigerator for a long time. Black salted beans are never eaten alone; they are used in a dish to season other foods.

Brown Bean
Sauce

原晒豉
Yüan Shai Shih

Ground Brown
Bean Sauce

磨原豉
Mo Yüen Shih

Brown bean sauce is made from fermented soybeans and wheat flour mixed with salt and water. The beans in the sauce may be either ground or left whole. To this basic bean sauce, spice and other seasonings are added, creating many varieties. Seasonings and spices are added to a bean sauce in different proportions in different regions of China. In Szechuan, large amounts of hot peppers and crushed Szechuan peppercorns are added; in the northern provinces, garlic and scallions are used; in Chekiang and Kiangsu, moderate amounts of sugar are used; and in Canton, large amounts of sugar, garlic, and spices are added. There are no set rules as to the amount of seasonings or spices added to a bean sauce; it is a question of personal taste. Many types of bean sauce can be made, each having a slightly different flavor, but they are all made from the same base. Many people prefer to use a plain sauce in order to have control over the taste; seasonings and spices then may be added according to the desires of the cook. Bean sauces are packed in many different types and sizes of cans and jars. If the sauce is canned, it should be transferred to a dry, rustproof container and kept in the refrigerator. It will not spoil for a long time. Bean sauce can be found in many Oriental food stores.

Hoisin Sauce

海鮮醬

Hai Hsien
Chiang

Hoisin sauce is a ground bean sauce to which sugar, garlic, and other flavorings have been added. It is the most popular commercially prepared flavored bean sauce. It is used for cooking, or very often as a dip for deep-fried batter-dipped vegetables. It should be stored in the same manner as other bean sauces.

Sesame Paste

芝蔴醬

Chih Ma Chiang

In the United States sesame paste is not easily available, but peanut butter mixed with sesame oil is sometimes used as a substitute. In northern China sesame paste is used to make dressings, and in cooking for its flavor and its richness in taste and texture.

Sesame Oil

蔴油

Ma Yu

Chinese sesame oil has a strong, nutlike, aromatic fragrance. In the northern regions of China it is used as a cooking oil, but generally it is used to flavor soups and hot or cold dishes. Adding a few drops of sesame oil to a dish that is ready to be served gives it a special flavor. Middle Eastern sesame oil has a paler color and is made from raw sesame seeds. It has a completely different flavor and is unsuitable for Chinese cooking. Sesame oil is available in most Oriental food shops. It should be stored in the refrigerator to prevent it from becoming rancid.

Ginger

薑

Chiang

Young Ginger

子薑

Tzu Chiang

Matured Ginger

老薑

Lao Chiang

Ginger is a rhizome. As the rootstock grows, it spreads underground with small lobes growing to the size of small potatoes. There are usually three, four, or five lobes in a chain. This is why gingerroot is sometimes called a hand of ginger; it looks like the knuckles of fingers. When young, each lobe has a sprouting point that is pinkish in color. The remainder of the lobe is pale yellow with a tender skin. When the ginger is left in the ground to mature, its peel becomes a beige color. The inside color varies from light yellow to pale yellowish green. It has a sharp aroma and is used to flavor salads and vegetables. It is not usually used in cooking clear, light, or delicately flavored soups. Only a small amount is necessary for seasoning. A chunk weighing about two ounces can last a long time if properly stored in the refrigerator. Moisture will rot the ginger. When it is left uncovered, it will shrivel until it is too hard to use. The best way to store fresh gingerroot is to put it in a perforated plastic bag in the vegetable compartment of the refrigerator. Gingerroot will keep for a few months.

Coriander

香菜（芫茜）

Hsiang Ts'ai

Chinese cooks use coriander leaves as Western cooks use parsley. Coriander is an herb of the parsley family and its seed is used as a spice. It is sold by the bunch in Chinese markets. Store in the same manner as parsley.

Hot Chili Peppers

辣椒

La Chiao

There are many varieties of pepper and the degree of spiciness differs. When a recipe calls for hot peppers, you can use any kind of peppers that has a hot flavor, whatever suits your taste.

Hot Chili Pepper Oil

辣油

La Yu

Hot pepper oil is often added to noodles or filled dumplings to give an extra-spicy final touch. This hot pepper oil is made by simply frying any one of the pungent peppers in oil until the capsaicin is extracted from the peppers. The oil turns red and its taste becomes pungent. The pepper pods are removed and may be used in other dishes. The seasoned oil can be stored in a bottle and is ready for use whenever desired. Store the oil in the refrigerator to keep it from becoming rancid. Hot pepper oil can also be bought in Chinese groceries.

Rock Sugar

冰糖

Ping T'ang

Rock sugar is crystallized sugar, much like rock candy, but it is made from raw sugar, which gives the crystals a slight brownish tinge. It gives a dish rich color as well as a glossy appearance. To measure rock sugar, simply crush and measure with measuring spoons.

Star Anise

八角

Pa Chiao

Spices can make a simple dish interesting. The star anise is a spice grown only in China. The seed comes with a pod, and both are used for flavoring. It is different from the anise seed. It is often used to flavor pressed bean curd.

Szechuan Peppercorns

花椒

Hua Chiao

This peppercorn is different from ordinary black peppercorns. It is not peppery but it gives a numbing sensation to the tongue. It also has a distinct aroma after roasting in a frying pan. This peppercorn has dark red open husks. The seeds are not enclosed in hulls and are dark red, almost black.

Sweet Olive

桂花

K'uei Hua

K'uei hua (sweet olive) is a tiny yellow four-petaled flower that grows on the branch of the Chinese cassia tree. It blooms around the moon festival—fifteenth day of the eighth of the lunar calender. In China the blossoms are collected and preserved in salt and sugar. They are used for flavoring sweet dishes and sweet soups. In New Orleans this tree is used as an ornamental hedge.

Monosodium
Glutamate

味精
Wei-Ching

The Chinese call monosodium glutamate *wei-ching*, which translates literally as "the essence of taste." It is a chemical in the form of white granules, and looks very much like shiny table salt. In Japan, monosodium glutamate is present in almost every kind of prepared food. A good cook will never automatically add monosodium glutamate to every dish. Properly preparing and seasoning good-quality, fresh ingredients in the right combination eliminates the need for monosodium glutamate. However, certain vegetarian dishes are enhanced by it. One should never use *wei-ching* in large quantities; a pinch to ¼ teaspoon is sufficient, depending upon the size of the dish.

Index